Level 1 Certificate for IT Users
for City & Guilds

Word Processing

for Office XP

Level

1

Rosemarie Wyatt

Endorsed by

City&
Guilds

www.heinemann.co.uk
✓ Free online support
✓ Useful weblinks
✓ 24 hour online ordering

01865 888058

Heinemann
Inspiring generations

Heinemann Educational Publishers
Halley Court, Jordan Hill, Oxford OX2 8EJ
Part of Harcourt Education

Heinemann is the registered trademark of Harcourt Education Limited

© Rosemarie Wyatt, 2004

First published in 2004
2007   2006
10   9   8   7   6   5   4   3

A catalogue record for this book is available from the British Library on request.

10-digit ISBN 0 435462 70 9
13-digit ISBN 978 0 435462 70 3

Acknowledgements
The authors and publishers would like to thank the following for permission to reproduce screenshots and marketing information: Microsoft (throughout book); Support for the Sick Newborn and their Parents (page 71, Example H); Newbury Spring Festival, Direct Line Insurance plc (page 72, Example J); Windermere Marina Village Ltd (page 73, Example K).

The publishers have made every effort to trace the copyright holders, but if they have inadvertently overlooked any, they will be pleased to make the necessary arrangements at the first opportunity.

All rights reserved. No part of this publication may be reproduced in any material form (including photocopying or storing it in any medium by electronic means and whether or not transiently or incidentally to some other use of this publication) without the prior permission of the copyright owner, except in accordance with the provisions of the Copyright, Designs and Patents Act 1988 or under the terms of a licence issued by the Copyright Licensing Agency Ltd, 90 Tottenham Court Road, London W1P 0LP. Applications for the copyright owner's written permission to reproduce any part of this publication should be addressed to the publisher.

Typeset by Techset, Gateshead
Printed and bound in Great Britain by Thomson Litho Ltd, Glasgow

Limit of liability/disclaimer of warranty
The accuracy and completeness of the information provided herein are not guaranteed or warranted to produce any particular results, and the advice and strategies contained herein may not be suitable for every individual.

Tel: 01865 888058   www.heinemann.co.uk

Contents

Introduction

City & Guilds e-Quals is an exciting new range of IT qualifications developed with leading industry experts. These comprehensive, progressive awards cover everything from getting to grips with basic IT to gaining the latest professional skills.

The range consists of both user and practitioner qualifications. User qualifications (Levels 1–3) are ideal for those who use IT as part of their job or in life generally, while Practitioner qualifications (Levels 2–3) have been developed for those who need to boost their professional skills in, for example, networking or software development.

e-Quals boasts on-line testing and a dedicated web site with news and support materials and web-based training. The qualifications reflect industry standards and meet the requirements of the National Qualifications Framework.

With e-Quals you will not only develop your expertise, you will gain a qualification that is recognised by employers all over the world.

Word processing was the firstly widely used applications software and made computers accessible to anyone who could use a keyboard. Word processing has come a long way. It is not just used for entering text and manipulating it to alter the content and the layout; it is also used for adding graphical elements, such as images, to pages. This book assumes the use of Microsoft Word for XP and is for beginners who have a basic knowledge of the mouse and keyboard.

The unit is organised into five outcomes. You will learn to:

- Plan and prepare to produce new documents
- Produce new documents
- Edit existing documents
- Check produced documents
- Save and print documents

It covers the specific skills and the underpinning knowledge for the outcomes of the Word Processing unit, although they are not dealt with separately or in the same order.

Each section covers several practical features as well as underpinning knowledge related to the unit outcomes. This is followed by skills practice and a chance to check your knowledge. Consolidation tasks give you the opportunity to put together skills and knowledge, and practice assignments complete your progress towards the actual assignment. As with all skills, practice makes perfect! Solutions to the knowledge checks and practice assignments can be found at the back of the book.

Your tutor will give you a copy of the outcomes, as provided by City & Guilds, so that you can sign and date each learning point as you master the skills and knowledge.

There is often more than one way of carrying out a task in Word, e.g. using the toolbar, menu or keyboard. Whilst this book may use one method, there are others, and alternatives are listed at the back in the 'Quick reference guide'. The tasks are designed to be worked through in order, as earlier tasks may be used in later sections. Good luck!

Section 1 | Getting started

You will learn to

- Use the mouse
- Load Word
- Identify parts of the Word document window
- Enter text into a document
- Save a file
- Print a file
- Close a file
- Create a new file
- Close Word
- Close down the computer

In this section you will learn the basics of word processing using the Microsoft application Word. You will familiarise yourself with the Word environment before going on to learn more specific skills.

Information: Using the mouse

Click	Press the left mouse button and release.
Double click	Press the left mouse button and release, twice, in quick succession.
Drag	For highlighting text hold down left mouse button and move across text to be selected, and release.
	Pointing to an object, hold down the left mouse button and move to the required position. Release the mouse button.

Information: Word

Word is part of the Microsoft Office suite. It has a graphical user interface (or GUI) which makes it easy for you to use. The use of icons (little images) and buttons help you to select the commands you want to carry out. If you are not sure what a button means, rest the mouse pointer over it and a screen tip will appear to explain. Whilst Word has many advanced features, it does not take long to get going, so let's get started.

Load is the commonly used term for starting up.

Task 1.1 Load Word

The first thing you must do after switching on your computer is to start up or load Word.

Method

1 Switch on your computer.
2 If you are using a network you will need a user ID and a password to log on. Check with your tutor.
3 Wait for the Windows desktop to appear.
4 Move the mouse pointer over the **Start** button on the **taskbar** and click the left mouse button – a menu appears (Figure 1.1). Your version may look slightly different to this depending on the programs available to you.

Figure 1.1 Loading Word

5 Move the mouse up the menu to **All Programs** and click the left button – another menu appears to the right.
6 Move the mouse to **Microsoft Word** and click the left button to load Word. Depending on how your system is set up, you may need to select Office XP first.
7 The Word document window should appear.

After you have used the Microsoft Word program for the first time, it should appear in the list on the left-hand side of the Start menu.

If a document window does not appear like the one below, click on the **New** button 🗋 on the left of the Standard toolbar at the top of the screen.

Information: Identify parts of the Word document window

Your screen may look slightly different to the one below.

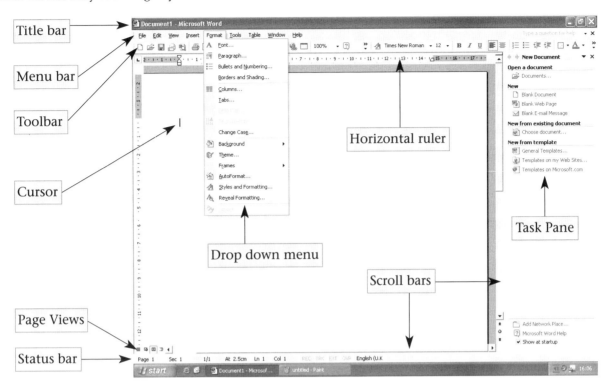

Figure 1.2 The document window

- **Title bar** This displays the name of the current document. The default (or automatic) filename is **Document 1**. (**Hint**: A default setting is one automatically preset by Word but which can usually be changed.)
- **Menu bar** Menus can be selected by using the mouse or keyboard. Each menu drops down to give further options. Initially a list of basic options appears followed a few seconds later by a full list. This list will change according to the items you have most recently selected. You can click on ☒ at the bottom of a menu to expand the list of options.

Figure 1.3 The toolbar

- **Toolbar** This features shortcut buttons for frequently used actions such as Print. If you position the mouse over a button and wait, a Screen Tip will appear giving an explanation of its function (Figure 1.3).
- The **Standard toolbar** is, by default, combined with the **Formatting toolbar**, which is used for changing the appearance of your text, e.g. making it bold. Both of these toolbars hold the more frequently used buttons but can be expanded to show more by clicking on **Toolbar Options** »

Some users prefer to work with both the full Standard and Formatting toolbars displayed. For the purpose of this book it would be helpful to see both. To do this:

1 Click on the **View** menu, select **Toolbars** and then **Customize**.
2 Click on the **Options** tab.
3 Click to add a tick in the box entitled **Show Standard and Formatting toolbars on two rows**.
4 Click on **Close**.

- **Horizontal ruler** This shows the position of text and graphics and aids accurate placement of objects on the page. There is also a **Vertical ruler** down the left side of the document window in Print Layout View.
- **Scroll bars** These allow you to move quickly through a document by scrolling the page up or down, or from side to side. Drag the grey bar vertically or horizontally as required on the scroll bar or click on the single arrow at the end of each scroll bar to move the page.
- **Cursor** This shows the position text will appear.
- **Status bar** This gives information on the page number and cursor position.
- **Page View icons** These allow different methods of viewing the page. These views can also be accessed via the **View** menu. For now, work in Normal View which is best for straightforward text entry and editing. Click on **View** menu and select **Normal**.
- **Task pane** On the right hand side of the screen, this opens automatically for certain tasks. It can be opened (select **Task pane** from the **View menu**) and closed as required.

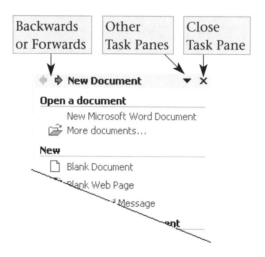

Figure 1.4 Task pane

Information

Before entering text using any word processor there are some basic points you need to know:

- **Word wrap** When keying in text never press Enter at the end of a line *within* a paragraph to move on to the next, as Word will automatically do this when necessary. This feature is called **word wrap** or **text wrap**.
- **Paragraph spacing** Paragraphs are used to break up text into logical sections. Always leave a line space between paragraphs by pressing the **Enter** key twice at the end of a paragraph and after headings (Figure 1.5).
- **Text spacing** Leave one space between each word by pressing the **spacebar** (the long bar at the bottom of the keyboard) once. It is usual to leave one space after a comma and one or two at the end of a sentence, but always be consistent.
  Capital letters To key in a capital letter, hold down the **Shift key** (Figure 1.6) and key in the letter. (Another **Shift key** is located below the **Enter** key.) To type several letters in capitals, press the **Caps Lock** key first. Press it again to release.
- **Other characters** To key in characters on the upper part of a key, e.g. above the numbers, ! and £ etc, hold down the **Shift key** and the required character.

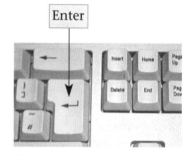

Figure 1.5 Enter key

Figure 1.6 Shift keys and Caps Lock

Task 1.2 — Enter text into the document

Notice how the cursor (a small black vertical line) is flashing at the point on the page where the text will appear.

Method

1   Key in the text below. If you make a mistake do not try to change it now. At the end of the line carry on typing – Word will automatically move on to the next line. Do not worry if the lines end at a different point to those in the example. Ignore any wavy lines that may appear under some words.

Nowadays anybody can word process. You do not have to be a good typist although it does help. Once you have keyed your text into a document you can format it, which means you can change the way the words look, for example increase their size. You can also edit it by changing the words themselves, for instance deleting words, inserting words or moving them around.

2   The cursor now appears where the text finishes – ready for more text to be entered if required. Press **Enter** twice and key in your full name.

Task 1.3 — Save the file

When you save a document it is known as a file, but generally both terms are used to mean the same thing. Always use a filename that reflects the contents so you can identify it later. Filenames can comprise upper or lower case letters, numbers or other characters except / \ > < * ? | :.

Method

1   Click on **Save** button 💾

2   The **Save As** dialogue box appears (Figure 1.7).

The **Save in** box indicates where the file will be saved. By default this will be to My Documents or to an area of a network assigned to you. Later you will save to other locations.

3   Click in the **File Name** box. Notice that the first few words of the file appear as a suggested name. Delete this by pressing **Delete** (Figure 1.8) and key in **Word processing** as the filename.

4   Click on **Save**.

Notice how the filename appears in the blue **title bar** at the top of the window.

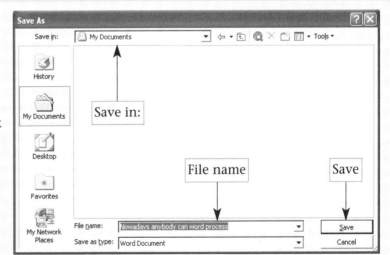

Figure 1.7 Save As dialogue box

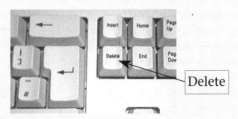

Figure 1.8 Delete

Task 1.4 | Print the file

Method

Click on the **Print** button 🖨 One copy of your file is sent to the printer.

Task 1.5 | Close the file

Method

Click on the **File** menu – select **Close**.

Task 1.6 | Create a new document, enter text, save, print, close

Method

1 Click on the **New** document button 🗋
2 Key in the following text. Do not worry about any errors. You can correct them later.

Remember:

Press Enter twice after a heading and at the end of a paragraph.

Hint:

Leave one space either side of a dash – as here, and no spaces either side of a hyphen as in accident-free.

> WORKING SAFELY
>
> Whether working at home, the office or in college, most accidents are caused by carelessness.
>
> If everybody takes prevention seriously and is aware of possible hazards then there is less chance of accidents happening.
>
> When sharing your workspace with others simple preventative measures can be taken to make sure you work tidily and do not leave folders, bags and boxes etc lying around. You might know your bag is on the floor, but do not forget your colleague who may be carrying something or looking elsewhere and trip over it! Working safely does not mean just thinking about yourself – be aware for the sake of others. Help to keep your workplace accident-free.

3 Save the file as **Working Safely**.
4 Print and close the file.

Task 1.7 | Close Word

Method

Click on **File** menu – select **Exit**.

Task 1.8   Close down the computer

Method

1   On a home or standalone computer, click on **Start** menu (Figure 1.9).
2   Click on **Turn Off Computer**.

Hint:

When working on a network, never switch off at the mains socket unless told to, because you may switch off other users' computers.

Hint:

To improve your basic word processing skills, whenever you have spare time, practise keying in text using copy from newspapers, books or magazines. Remember to save regularly and use sensible filenames that reflect the content.

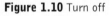

Figure 1.9 Start – Turn off

3   Click Turn Off as in Figure 1.10.
4   Switch off.

On a network computer you must
Log off – check with your supervisor/tutor.
Make a note of what you have to do.

Figure 1.10 Turn off

→ Practise your skills 1

1   Load Word, open a new document and enter text as follows. Do not worry about any errors. You will correct them later.

> WORD PROCESSING BASICS
>
> You are now entering text onto the screen using word processing software. Watch how the cursor moves across the screen as you key in text. Notice that when you get to the end of each line, a new line is started automatically. Any word that enters into the margin area running down the right-hand side of the screen is moved onto the next line. This feature is called word wrap or text wrap.
>
> As well as avoiding a break in the flow of text entry, it leaves the text on the screen in a flexible form that means the document layout can be later changed very easily. For instance, the margins could be changed.
>
> It is important therefore to remember not to press Enter at the end of each line, so that the document format – the layout – can be altered.

2   Save the document with the filename **WP Basics**.
3   Print.
4   Close the file and exit Word.

Information

You may see wavy lines below some words. Ignore these for now.

→ Practise your skills 2

Load Word, open a new document and enter text as follows. Do not worry about any errors. You can correct them later.

Hint:

To key in the euro € symbol, press **Alt Gr** (to the right of the space bar) and **4** together.

THE EURO

The euro is the single currency of the European Union. The euro symbol is € and is derived from the Greek letter of the alphabet, epsilon. It also represents the first letter of the word 'Europe'. The two lines across the symbol indicate stability within the euro area. EUR is the official abbreviation for the euro.

Bank notes and coins came into general circulation in January 2002 in those countries that decided to adopt it and they are legal tender in any of the member countries. The new currency consists of seven different banknotes and eight different coins and they replaced those of the participating countries. The banknotes are identical but whilst one side of the coins is the same for all countries, the reverse side is specific to each country reflecting a feature of that nation.

To help the blind and partially sighted, different size notes have been produced and there are tactile marks around the edge of the larger notes. The value of notes is printed in large, bold figures, which helps fully sighted people as well.

The coins vary in size, weight and thickness and the edges of coins are also different.

1 Save the document with the filename **The Euro**.
2 Print.
3 Close the file and exit from Word.
4 If your working session is finished, close down your computer.

→ Check your knowledge

1 What appears in the title bar?
2 What is word wrap?
3 What should you do after a heading and at the end of a paragraph?
4 What should you remember when naming a file?
5 What key do you press to type several capital letters together?
6 How do you start a new Word document?
7 How do you key in the euro symbol €?
8 Where is the name of a file displayed onscreen?
9 How many spaces should you leave at the end of a sentence?
10 What are meant by the terms hard and soft copies?

Editing

You will learn to

- Open an existing file
- Check your work
- Use the spellcheck
- Quick save a file
- Move around a file
- Carry out basic editing – delete and insert text
- Check paragraph and character spacing
- Join and split paragraphs
- Use Undo and Redo
- Use Save As

Editing means changing the content of a file. In this section you will carry out some basic editing skills such as delete (remove) and insert (add) letters and words.

Task 2.1   Open existing file

Method

1   Switch on your computer and load Word.

2   Click on the **Open** button 📂

3   Select **Word Processing**.
4   Click on **Open** (Figure 2.1).
5   The file opens.

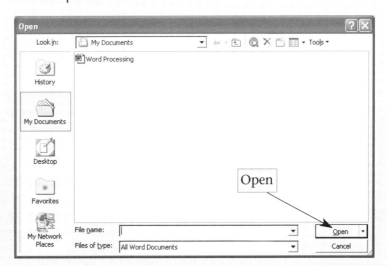

Figure 2.1 Open existing file

Information: Checking your work

When preparing any document it is important that the end result should be accurate; it is therefore essential to get into the habit of ensuring this right from the start. **Spellchecking** is one way of helping you to achieve this.

Spellchecking

Word has an automatic spellcheck that checks each word of your document against an in-built dictionary. As you enter text, any word the spellchecker does not recognise will appear on screen with a red wavy line underneath, e.g. your own name. This does not necessarily mean that it is wrong, rather that the spellcheck does not recognise it. The word may not be in the dictionary or it may be a proper name. Do not totally rely on the spellcheck as it does not spot words that are correctly spelt but used in the wrong context, e.g. 'I am going <u>four</u> a walk', or 'I am going <u>two</u> go with <u>ewe</u>'. It does not check whether your sentences make sense either, or whether they convey the right meaning. Use the spellcheck, but always read through your work carefully too, before and after printing. This is called proofreading – you will learn more about this in Section 8. The spellcheck works in conjunction with a Grammar checker that underlines words that may be grammatically incorrect with a green wavy line. Corrections can be made, if necessary, in the same way as the spellcheck.

Task 2.2	Spellcheck the document

Method

1 Click on the Spelling and Grammar button.
2 The Spelling and Grammar dialogue box appears (Figure 2.2) unless you have no errors!

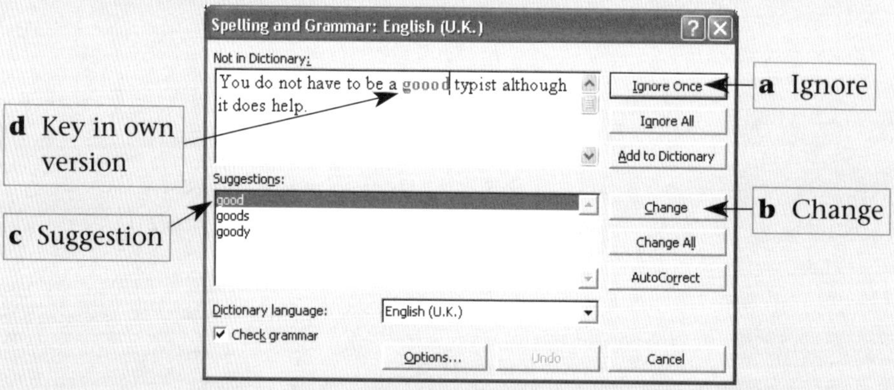

Figure 2.2 Spellcheck

3 The spellchecker scans through your document, stopping at any words it does not recognise and displays them in red in the spellcheck window.
4 Either:
  a Click on **Ignore Once** if you are satisfied with the spelling, or
  b Click on **Change** to accept the highlighted suggested spelling, or
  c Click on another **Suggestion** in the list and then click on **Change**, or
  d Key in your own version of the word and click on **Change**.
5 The spellcheck continues through the document, repeating the process. When it has finished, a message confirms the spellcheck is complete. Click **OK**.

If you had no errors in your document, return to this section when you next need to use the spellcheck.

6 Print the file.

Hint:

It is also possible to **Add** words to the dictionary that you use frequently, such as proper names.

Remember:

From now on you should always use the spellcheck and proofread your work.

Task 2.3 — Quick save the file

Once a file has been saved and named, click on the **Save** button 🖫 to resave it at any time. Any amendments are saved, overwriting the original file. It is good practice to save your work every ten minutes using this method, in case a system error or power failure occurs. You would then only lose work up to your last save.

Method

Click on **Save** button 🖫

Information: Move around a file

There are several ways of moving around a document. Try these now.

- **Use the mouse**   As you move the mouse over the text it takes on the appearance of an I-beam. Move it to the required position and click the left mouse button once. The cursor will appear at that point.

Figure 2.3 Moving around

- **Use the keyboard**   Towards the right of the main keyboard is a bank of four arrow keys (Figure 2.3). Pressing one of the keys causes the cursor to move up, down, left or right accordingly. Holding a key down speeds up the movement.
- **Use keyboard shortcuts**   You can move quickly around a file using these shortcuts on the keyboard. First locate Ctrl (Control) in the bottom left corner of the keyboard, and Home, End, Page Up and Page Down (Figure 2.3).

Home	To move to the start of a line
End	To move to the end of a line
Ctrl + Home	To move to the start of a document file
Ctrl + End	To move to the end of a document file
Page Up	Moves up one screen
Page Down	Moves down one screen

The last two actions are useful when working with long files, as is the use of the scroll bars – see Section 1 Page 3.

> ## Information: Editing
>
> Editing means to change the content of a document. This might involve altering words or characters by deleting, inserting, copying or moving them around. Graphics and images can also be edited.

Task 2.4 Delete text

Characters can be deleted to the left of the cursor position or to the right.

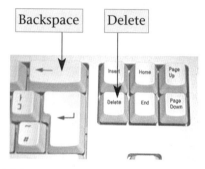

Figure 2.4 Backspace and delete

- **To delete to the left of the cursor** Press the Backspace key (Figure 2.4).
- **To delete to the right of the cursor** Press the Delete key.

> ## Method
>
> I Position the cursor directly after the word **good** in the second sentence. Press the **Backspace** key once. Repeat until the word **good** and the space in front of it have been deleted.
>
> 2 Position the cursor directly in front of the word **your** in the third sentence. Press the **Delete** key once. Repeat until the word **your** and the space following it have been deleted.
>
> 3 Save the file.

Task 2.5 Insert text

Text can be inserted by positioning the cursor where the text is required and keying it in. The text to the right of the cursor moves across making space for the new word/s. If this should not happen and the new text overtypes the existing text, check to see if **OVR** appears in black on the status bar (bottom of the screen), indicating overtype mode is on. If it is, double click to dim it (Figure 2.5).

Overtype mode is on

Figure 2.5 Overtype

Method

1   Position the cursor directly In front of the word **anybody** in the first line. Key in the word **practically** and press the spacebar to leave a space.
2   Position the cursor directly in front of the word **does** in the second sentence. Key in the word **certainly** and leave a space.
3   Position the cursor directly in front of the full stop after the word **size** at the end of the third sentence. Press the spacebar and key in **or make them bold**.
4   Spellcheck your document and proofread the document onscreen making any necessary corrections.
5   Save your file.

Task 2.6   Check paragraph and character spacing

Another way of checking your work is to show the paragraph markers (where you have pressed Enter) and character spacing (where you have pressed the spacebar). This is particularly useful when you have been editing.

Method

1   Click on the **Show/Hide** button ¶ on the toolbar. Each time Enter has been pressed is shown by ¶ and each space is shown by a raised dot ·.
2   Check to make sure there are no unnecessary or missing spaces.
3   Check to make sure there are only paragraph markers at the end of each paragraph and between paragraphs.
4   Make any necessary amendments.
5   Click **Show/Hide** button to hide markers.
6   Save and close the file.

Hint:

It is always a good idea to save your file before printing and after making significant changes to a document.

Task 2.7   Join and split paragraphs

When editing documents you may be required to change where the paragraphs break, to split a paragraph up or to join two paragraphs together.

Method

1 Click on **Open** button 🗁
2 Select the file **Working Safely**.
3 Press **Open**.
4 To join the first two paragraphs together, position the cursor immediately before the first word of the second paragraph **If** (Figure 2.6).

> If everybody takes prevention seriously and is aware of possible hazards then there is less chance of accidents happening.

Figure 2.6 Join two paragraphs

5 Press **Backspace** twice.
6 Press the **spacebar** to ensure you leave space/s after the full stop.
7 To split the last paragraph into two, position the cursor directly in front of the first letter of the intended new paragraph, in this case **Working** (Figure 2.7).

> might know your bag is on the floor, but do not forget your colleague who may be carrying something or looking elsewhere and trip over it! Working safely does not mean just thinking about yourself - be aware for the sake of others. Help to keep your workplace accident-free.

Figure 2.7 Splitting a paragraph

8 Press **Enter** twice.
9 Check your work by using **Show/Hide**.
10 Use the spellcheck and proofread your work onscreen.
11 Save, print and close the file.

You should have three paragraphs.

Task 2.8 | Use Undo and Redo

Everybody makes mistakes sometimes and you may, for example, delete some text or split a paragraph and then change your mind. Word has a very useful feature that remembers the last few changes you made and allows you to reverse them. It will let you **undo** a change and also allow you to **redo** it! Each time you click on Undo it will take you back one more stage (Figure 2.8). Clicking on the down arrow at the side of the Undo button allows you to select a particular action, but beware as it takes you back to that stage in the document when you performed it.

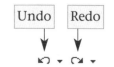

Figure 2.8 Undo and Redo

Method

1 Open the file **Word Processing**.
2 Delete any word.
3 Click on **Undo**.
4 Split the paragraph into two so the new paragraph starts **Once you have** ...
5 Click on **Undo**.
6 Now click on **Redo**.
7 Do not save or close the file.

Information: Save As

So far you have used the Save button to save files. The first time a file is saved you must name it. When you subsequently save it by the same method, you are not prompted for a name as it already has one. Any changes you have made overwrite the original.

There may, however, be occasions when you wish to save a new version of a file with any amendments but keep the original document intact. This is when you use **Save As**, meaning you **Save** a file **As** something else, i.e. by another name. The new name can be similar or completely different, but of course should always reflect the content. **Save As** can also be used for saving a file to another location.

Task 2.9 — Save a file using a new name

You are going to save **Word Processing** with a new name to preserve the original. Note the existing filename in the title bar at the top of the screen before you do this.

Method

1   Using the open file **Word Processing** select **Save As** from the **File** menu.
2   Key in the filename **Word Processing 2**.
3   Click on **Save**. Note the new filename in the title bar.
4   Close the file.

→ Practise your skills 1

1   Open the file **WP Basics**.
2   In the first sentence of the second paragraph after the words **later changed**, delete the words **very easily**.
3   In the first sentence of the second paragraph after the words **text entry**, delete the word **it** and replace it with **word wrap.**
4   In the last sentence of the first paragraph after the word **This**, insert the word **useful**.
5   Join the last two paragraphs to make one. Ensure a space is left between the two sentences.
6   Split the first paragraph up so that the new paragraph begins **Watch how** ...
7   Spellcheck.
8   Proofread onscreen including checking for paragraph and spacing errors.
9   Use **Save As** to save the file as **WP Basics 2** and print.
10   Close the file.

Remember:

Save regularly as you work.

→ Practise your skills 2

1. Open the file **The Euro**.
2. In the second sentence delete the words **of the alphabet**.
3. In the first sentence of the second paragraph delete the word **general**.
4. After the first sentence of the first paragraph ending **Union**, insert a new sentence **In theory this will make trade across Europe much easier**.
5. In the last sentence of the second paragraph insert the word **particular** in front of **feature**.
6. Split the second paragraph so the new paragraph begins **The new currency**.
7. Join the last two paragraphs together.
8. Spellcheck.
9. Proofread onscreen including checking for paragraph and spacing errors.
10. Use **Save As** to save the file as **European Currency** and print.
11. Close the file and exit from Word.
12. If your working session is finished, close down your computer.

→ Check your knowledge

1. What does the term editing mean?
2. How often should you save your work and why?
3. What is the difference between Save and Save As?
4. When should each be used?
5. How can you move the cursor quickly to the start of a line?
6. Why should you not rely on the spellcheck to spot all errors?
7. What is the purpose of Show/Hide?
8. What is overtype mode?
9. What is the difference between Backspace and Delete?
10. What is the function of these four toolbar buttons?

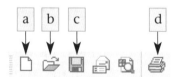

Figure 2.9

Section 3 — Selecting and formatting

You will learn to

- Select text
- Close a file without saving
- Spellcheck part of a document
- Consider appropriate text formatting
- Format text
  - ☐ Change font size and style
  - ☐ Enhance text
- Align text
- Change Print options

Formatting means to change the appearance of text. This might mean, for example, changing the size of words or making them bold. In this section you will first learn how to select text before you format it.

Information: Selecting text

There are many ways of altering the appearance of a document. This is often carried out by changing selected areas of text. It is therefore useful to look at ways of selecting text before going any further.

To select:	Method
One word	Double click on word (also selects the following space).
Several words	Press and drag the I-beam across several words and release (Figure 3.1).
A line	Click alongside line in left margin (Figure 3.2) (mouse pointer changes to an arrow pointing right).
A paragraph	Double click alongside paragraph in left margin.
A sentence	Hold down **Ctrl**. Click anywhere in sentence.
Whole document	Hold down **Ctrl** and click in left margin **or** choose Select All from Edit menu.
A block of text	Click cursor at start point, hold down **Shift**. Click cursor at end point.
To deselect	Click anywhere off the text.

Task 3.1   Select text

Method

1 Open the file **Working Safely**.
2 Position the cursor directly in front of the text to be selected – here it is the words **with others** in the second paragraph.
3 Hold down the left mouse button and drag the I-beam across both words and the following space. The text appears to be highlighted (Figure 3.1).

> When sharing your workspace with others simple preventative measures can be taken to make sure you work tidily and do not leave folders, bags and boxes etc lying around. You

Figure 3.1 Selecting text

4 Press **Delete** and then click on **Undo** to restore the text.
5 Click off the text to remove the highlighting.
6 Click in the left margin alongside the first line of the text in that paragraph (Figure 3.2).

> When sharing your workspace with others simple preventative measures can be taken to make sure you work tidily and do not leave folders, bags and boxes etc lying around. You might know your bag is on the floor, but do not forget your colleague who may be

Figure 3.2 Select a line

7 Press **Delete** and then click on **Undo**.
8 Try all the methods of selecting text in the table above. Press **Delete** and then **Undo** each time.
9 Close the file *without* saving. When prompted to save, click on **No** (Figure 3.3).

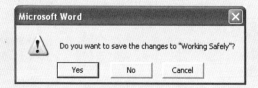

Figure 3.3 Close without saving

Hint:

From time to time rest your eyes by looking up and focusing into the distance.

Task 3.2   Spellcheck part of a document

You have already used the spellcheck for entire documents but part of a document can be checked by selecting it first.

Method

1 Open the file **Working Safely**.
2 Highlight the last two paragraphs.
3 Click on the spellcheck button.

The Spellcheck functions in exactly the same way as for entire documents but when it is complete, the following message appears:

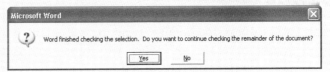

Figure 3.4 Spellcheck

4   Click on **No** in this instance.
5   Save the file and close.

Information: Format text – Text styles and enhancement

One of the main advantages of a word processing package is that it enables the user to present documents in an attractive way by formatting. This means that not only should they be more pleasing to look at but also more professional. Formatting might involve changing the size of text, the font style or enhancing particular key points to give them emphasis and make them stand out from the rest of the text. Here are some examples:

Font	Most fonts are either **serif** or **sans serif**. Serifs are little strokes at the ends of characters which sans serif characters do not have. The default font in Word is **Times New Roman** which is a serif font. **Arial** is an example of sans serif. Both fonts are suitable for standard business documents, although serif fonts are considered easier when reading lengthy documents. There are a huge number of fonts available, e.g. Comic Sans, Mistral, Verdana and Jokerman. They can be traditional, formal, serious, informal, fun, quirky, friendly etc. Choose carefully according to the message you have to convey.
Font size	Size 10 or 12 is the usual default size for body text but can be varied, especially for headings and subheadings and also for special purposes, e.g. advertisements. Font sizes are measured in points – the higher the number, the larger the font, e.g. 16 point, 18 point, 20 point. Different fonts can appear to be different sizes even set at the same size.
CAPITALS	Capitals are used to make words stand out, especially headings.
Bold	The term 'to embolden text' means to make it bold, which is heavier and darker than normal text. Bold is frequently used to make words more noticeable, especially headings.
Italics	Italics are also used for emphasis, usually within the main body of a document.
<u>Underline</u>	Underline is not used as much as bold, but is useful for giving emphasis to particular words in the main body of a document, and sometimes for headings.

When formatting documents, care should be taken to use appropriate methods for the particular document. Too many different forms of emphasis will detract from the message. See below:

Here is an **example** of the *misuse of formatting*. Too many <u>different</u> *fonts* have been used together with ***different*** sizes. The paragraph **LOOKS FAR TOO BUSY** and the reader will find it *<u>difficult</u>* to *read the words* let alone TAKE IN THE MEANING.

This is obviously an extreme example but illustrates the point. Consider also the following:

It is with regret that we have to announce the closure of our Watford branch resulting in a hundred and twenty redundancies.

Only one font has been used, but it is inappropriate for the serious message it is trying to communicate. Different fonts convey different messages, so always choose carefully.

You can see that the choice of font styles and sizes can have a major effect on the appearance and impact of a document, so bear the following points in mind:

- Ensure the font is appropriate for the document and will convey the right message.
- For standard business documents, Times New Roman and Arial (or similar) are considered 'safe'.
- As a general rule never use more than two fonts, or three at the most, in a document. Exceptions might be promotional material, which may particularly demand it.
- For normal continuous text, use size 10 or 12. Below 10 makes text difficult to read and above 12 is generally reserved for text emphasis or display purposes.
- Avoid too much emphasis and certainly too many different types of emphasis in one document.
- Use font style and size to give structure to a page by making main headings bigger than subheadings, which in turn should be bolder and possibly bigger than the main body of text.
- Ensure the document is legible.
- Consider housestyle if applicable. Most organisations have a housestyle that sets out which font/s and sizes should be used, ensuring consistency across all their documents.

Information

The **Formatting** toolbar holds the necessary buttons for fonts, size and emphasis.

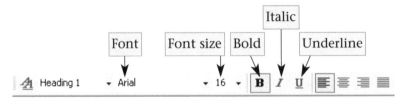

Figure 3.5 Formatting toolbar

- **To format text by changing font or font size** Select existing text and click on the arrow alongside either the font or font size to reveal a drop down list of fonts and sizes (Figure 3.6). You can also key in a size in between those offered, e.g. 11. For a choice of fonts scroll through the font list by clicking on the up and down scroll buttons (Figure 3.7).

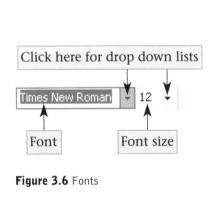

Figure 3.6 Fonts

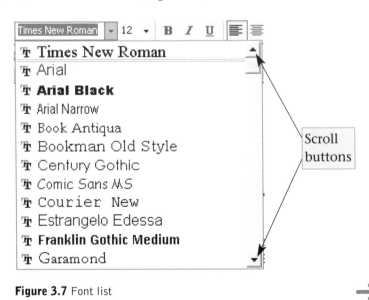

Figure 3.7 Font list

- **To format text by changing style of emphasis**
  Select existing text and click on Bold, Italics or Underline button as required (Figure 3.8).

  These options can also be chosen prior to keying in new text.

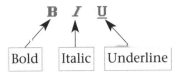

Figure 3.8 Emphasis

Task 3.3   Format and emphasise text

Method

1   Open a new file.
2   Key in the following text for an advertisement:

> Foremans Office Furniture
>
> Sale Now On
>
> Desks
> Chairs
> Cabinets
> Workstations
>
> Prices reduced by up to 25%
> While stocks last
>
> Visit our Cambridge showroom this week
>
> 234 Stockwell Road

3   Check your text using the spellcheck and by proofreading.
4   Save the file as **Foremans advert**.
5   Select the first line and click on the **Bold** button.
6   With the text still selected, click on the **Font** drop down list, scroll down and select the font **Impact**.
7   With the text still selected, click on the **Font size** drop down list and select **18**.
8   Select the remainder of the text and change to font style **Arial**.
9   Select **Sale Now On** and change to size **16**, **bold**.
10   Change **Prices reduced by up to 25%** to size **14**, **bold**.
11   Change **While stocks last** to **size 14**, **bold** and **underline**.
12   Check your work for errors.
13   Save the file, print and close the file.

Task 3.4   Change formatting

Method

1   Open the file **Foremans advert**.
2   Make formatting changes of your own choice.
3   Save the file using **Save As** with the name **Foremans advert 2**.
4   Print.
5   Close the file.

Information: Format text – Text alignment

Text is, by default, aligned to the left. This means that the left margin is straight but the right-hand side is 'ragged' – each line ending at a different point. This paragraph is an example of text that is **left aligned**. Left alignment is sometimes known as ragged right or unjustified.

This paragraph has **justified** margins, which means that the margins are straight on both sides. Word adjusts the words and spaces so that each line stretches across the page to end at the right margin. The exception is the last line of the paragraph, which would look odd if spaced across the page.

Normal continuous text is aligned left or justified. For long documents, left aligned text is considered to give maximum readability – look inside a few books to see.

Centred text is centred between left and right margin. It is not used for continuous text but may be used for headings or displaying text, e.g.

HERE IS A CENTERED HEADING

Aligned right causes each line to end at the right margin. It is not used as often as other alignments but might be used for display purposes or for an address in a personal letter, e.g.

23 Rawlinson Way

Luton

LU14 9JH

The **Formatting toolbar** also holds the necessary buttons for **alignment**.

- **To change alignment** Select existing text to be aligned and click on appropriate button. Alignment options can also be chosen prior to keying in new text.

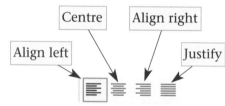

Figure 3.9 Alignment

Task 3.5 — Change text alignment – Centring

Method

1. Open the original file **Foremans advert**.
2. Select all the text and click on the **Centre** button.
3. Use **Save As** to name the file **Foremans Advert 3**.
4. Print and close the file.

Task 3.6 — Change text alignment – Centring and justifying

Method

1. Open the file **Working Safely**.
2. Select the heading, make it bold and click on the **Centre** button.
3. Use **Save As** to name the file **Working Safely 2**.
4. Select the remaining paragraphs and click on the **Justify** button.
5. Use **Save As** to name the file **Working Safely 3**.

Do not close the file yet.

Information: Print options

So far you have printed one copy of a document using the Print button, but there is another way to print that gives you more choice. The Print dialogue box is found by selecting Print from the File menu.

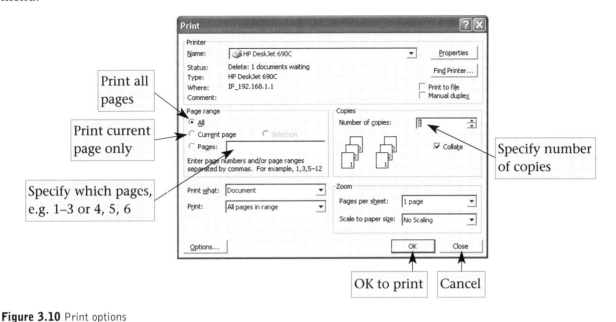

Figure 3.10 Print options

Task 3.7   Use print options

Method

1   Select **Print** from the **File** menu (Figure 3.10). Wait a few seconds for the full menu to appear.
2   Click in the **Number of copies** box and key in **2**.
3   Click **OK**.
4   Print and close the file.

→ Practise your skills 1

1   Open the file **European Currency**.
2   Select all the text and change the font to Arial size 11. (If text is already Arial, change it to Times New Roman.)
3   Embolden the euro symbol € in the first paragraph.
4   Underline the last sentence of the first paragraph beginning **EUR** . . .
5   Select the entire document and justify the margins.
6   Centre the heading and make it bold size 14.
7   Save the file as **European Currency 2** and print.
8   Change the alignment for the entire document to left align.
9   Print 2 copies.
10   Close the file *without saving*.

→ Practise your skills 2

1. Open a new file and key in the following text for an advertisement. Press Enter twice between lines where you think it is appropriate:

> Contemporary Window Dressings
> Curtains and Blinds made-to-measure
> In the comfort of your own home
> You choose
> We measure
> We make
> We fit
> Satisfaction guaranteed
> Call us now on 0191 768 452

2. Save the file as **Curtains and Blinds**.
3. Check your work.
4. Choose suitable fonts, sizes, enhancement and alignment.
5. Save again.
6. Print 2 copies and close the file.
7. Close down Word and close down your system.

→ Check your knowledge

1. What is the quick method of selecting a single word?
2. What is the term used to describe text that is selected?
3. What does the term formatting mean?
4. What is the default font and size on your system?
5. What is justified alignment?
6. What alignment is considered best for readability?
7. What size font is considered best for readability?
8. What is the difference between serif and sans serif fonts?
9. Name a font suitable for business documents (other than your default).
10. Make a list of all the things you should consider when formatting text, considering font, size, emphasis and alignment.

Consolidation 1

1 Start up your computer and load Word (log in if using a network).

2 Start a new file and key in the following text:

FENG SHUI

The words Feng Shui mean wind and water. Feng Shui has been practised in mainland China for several thousand years. This is a system of arranging your surroundings to live in harmony with them.

It is believed that our surroundings can influence our lives, affecting our health and wealth as well as relationships.

Followers of Feng Shui consider very carefully in which direction their house should face and how the furniture should be arranged. Everything should be designed to be harmonious with nature, and there should be no straight lines (only curves). This is to allow the movement of Ch'i or universal energy, which brings vitality and life into your home. Some people in the West live by the rules of Feng Shui whilst others are sceptical. What do you think?

Hint:

Use the shift key to type the brackets ( ) and question mark ?
Leave no space between brackets and the word/s they enclose (as here). Apostrophe ' is below @ symbol.

3 Check the file using the spellcheck and by proofreading.

4 Save the file as **Feng Shui** and print.

5 In the first sentence before the word **mean**, insert the word **literally**.

6 In the second paragraph insert the word **our** in front of **relationships**.

7 In the second sentence of the first paragraph delete the word **mainland**.

8 In the first sentence of the third paragraph delete the word **very**.

9 Join the first and second paragraphs to make one.

10 Split the last paragraph so the new paragraph begins **Some people** . . .

11 Change the font for the entire document to a script style font, e.g. Bradley Hand, and the font size to 14.

12 Justify the document.

13 Embolden the heading, centre it and increase the size to 16.

14 Proofread the document and particularly check for any spacing errors.

15 Save the file as **Feng Shui 2** and print.

16 Change alignment for the entire document to left align.

17 Print 2 copies and close *without saving*.

Saving and opening files using specified locations

You will learn to

- Create a folder
- Save files to a floppy disk
- Save files to a folder
- Open files from existing folders

In this section you will find out how to organise your files by saving them into different folders and to floppy disk. You will need a floppy disk for this section and for later sections.

Information

All files saved so far have been saved to a file store area called **My Documents** on the hard disk (called **C: drive**) of a single standalone computer, or it might be called **My Work** on a network (possibly **N: drive** but this may vary – check with your supervisor/tutor). You will soon have created many files and it is useful to save them into folders, just as you might organise paper files in a filing cabinet, as this helps you to find them later. Folders should be given relevant names, just as files should. Here you will use a name relevant to the section of the book.

> **Remember:**
>
> Files and folders should always have names relevant to their contents.

Task 4.1 — Save a file into a new folder

Method

1   Open a new file and type in your name and address.
2   Select **Save As** from the File menu.
3   Click on **Create New Folder** (Figure 4.1).

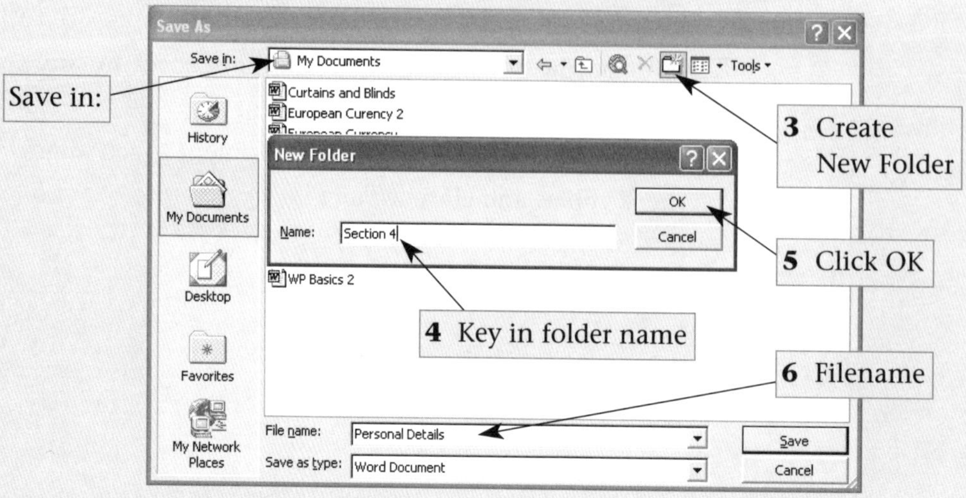

Save in:

3 Create New Folder

4 Key in folder name

5 Click OK

6 Filename

Figure 4.1 Save to a new folder

4   Key in the folder name **Section 4**.
5   Click **OK**. Note the **Save in:** box should now read **Section 4** to show the file will be saved into this new folder.
6   Key in the filename **Personal Details** and click on **Save**.
7   Key in your telephone number at the end of your document.
8   Select **Save As** from the **File** menu.
9   Key in the filename **Personal Details 2** and click on **Save**.
    Notice it will automatically be saved into Section 4.

NOTE: When creating a new folder ensure that the **Save in:** box reads **My Documents**.

Information

You may wish to save a file to a location other than the current folder, e.g. back to My Documents.

Task 4.2 Save a file to My Documents

Method

1   Using the same file, select **Save As** from the **File** menu.
2   Click on **My Documents** in the side bar (Figure 4.2). My Documents appears in **Save in:** box.

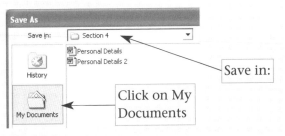

Figure 4.2 Changing folders

3   Key in filename **Personal Details 3** and click on Save.

Task 4.3 Save a file into an existing folder

Method

1   Using the same file, select **Save As** from the **File** menu.
2   Double click on the **Section 4** folder. Section 4 appears in the **Save in:** box.
3   Key in filename **Personal Details 4** and click on Save.

Hint:

Use sensible names for folders that will help you find your files.

Information

Sometimes you might also want to save a file onto a floppy disk as a backup copy in case something happens to the original, or you may want to take the file elsewhere. The floppy disk drive is called **A: drive**.

Task 4.4	Save a file to a floppy disk

Note:

A floppy disk can hold up to 70 pages of plain text.

Method

I   Insert a floppy disk into the disk drive with the label uppermost and nearest to you (Figure 4.3).

Figure 4.3 Inserting a floppy disk

2   Push it gently but firmly into the drive.
3   Using the same file, select **Save As** from the **File** menu.
4   Click on the down arrow alongside the **Save in**: box (Figure 4.4).

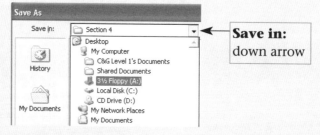

Figure 4.4 Select A: drive

5   Click on **3½ Floppy (A:)**.
6   Key in the filename **Personal Details 4** and click on **Save**.
7   Close the file.
8   When the disk drive light goes out, push the small button directly below the drive (usually) and the disk is released. (Make sure you do not press the power button which may be nearby!)

Hint:

Never take a floppy disk out while the disk drive light is on.

Information

Floppy disks are fairly robust but should be handled carefully and stored in a disk box. Keep them away from food, drink and smoke, and do not expose them to extremes in temperature.

Task 4.5 — Open an existing file from a folder

Method

1   Click on Open 📂

2   If **My Documents** is not displayed in the **Look in:** box, click on **My Documents** in the side bar (Figure 4.5).

Figure 4.5 Look in

3   Double click on **Section 4**.
4   Click on the file **Personal Details 2**.
5   Click on **Open** (or double click on the filename).
6   Close the file.

Hint:

When saving or opening files to and from different locations always start off in **My Documents** (click in side bar in Open/Save dialogue box – Figure 4.5) if unsure where you are!

→ Practise your skills 1

Practise saving and opening files to different locations.

1   Open a new file and key in your favourite colour.
2   Save the file as **Colours** directly into **My Documents**.
3   Use **Save As** to save the file as **Colours 2** into the **Section 4 folder**.
4   Insert a floppy disk.
5   Use **Save As** to save the file as **Colours 3** onto a **floppy disk**.
6   Close the file.
7   Open the file **Colours** from **My Documents**.
8   Close the file.
9   Open the file **Colours 2** from **Section 4 folder**.
10   Close the file.
11   Open the file **Colours 3** from **floppy disk**.
12   Use **Save As** to save the file using the same name (i.e. **Colours 3**) into My Documents.
13   Close the file.
14   Remove the floppy disk.

→ Check your knowledge

1   What is C: drive?
2   What is A: drive?
3   What is the purpose of a folder?
4   What must you wait for before removing a floppy disk?
5   What is a backup copy?

Tables and lists

You will learn to

- Recognise different types of tab
- Create and amend tables using tabs
- Create and amend tables using the Table facility
- Create and amend lists using Bullets and Numbering

Tables are used to set out information in columns and rows so that it is easy to read. In this section you will find out how to do this as well as how to set out lists.

Information: Tabulation

Tabulation is the arrangement of text and numbers in columns and rows. This can be achieved either by using **Tabs** or Word's **Table** feature.

Tabs

Tab stops can be set across the page at points where you wish to line up text. There are several different types of tab that affect the way this happens. The most commonly used are:

L Left tab

⌐ Right tab

⊥ Centre tab

⊥· Decimal tab

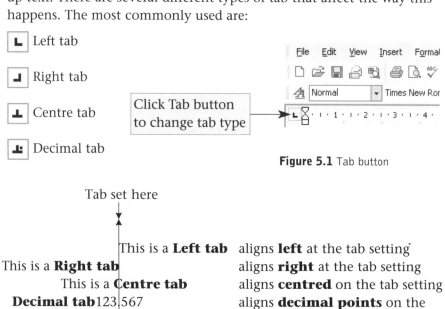

Click Tab button to change tab type

Figure 5.1 Tab button

Tab set here

This is a **Left tab**   aligns **left** at the tab setting
This is a **Right tab**   aligns **right** at the tab setting
This is a **Centre tab**   aligns **centred** on the tab setting
Decimal tab123.567   aligns **decimal points** on the tab setting

By default, left tabs are set every 1.27 cm (½ inch) across the page. When a new tab is set, the default tabs to the left of it are cleared.

Remember:

A default setting is one that is automatically set but which can usually be changed.

Task 5.1 — Create a table using tabs

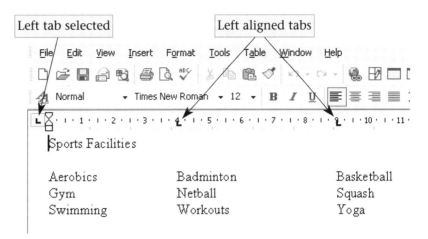

Figure 5.2 Table using tabs

Method

1   Open a new file.
2   Key in the heading **Sports Facilities** (Figure 5.2). Press Enter twice.
3   Check left tab is selected on the Tab button, click on ruler at 4 cm to set a tab. Notice tab marker appears on the ruler.
4   Click on ruler at 9 cm to set a tab.
5   Key in **Aerobics** and press **Tab** key (Figure 5.3).
6   Key in **Badminton** and press **Tab** key.
7   Key in **Basketball** and press **Enter** for a new line.
8   Repeat for the next two lines pressing **Tab** to move across the page and **Enter** to start a new line.
9   Save the file as **Sports Facilities** into a new folder called **Section 5** in My Documents.
10 Spellcheck and proofread. Resave if necessary.
11 Print and close.

Figure 5.3 Tab key

Task 5.2 — Create a table using different tab types

Method

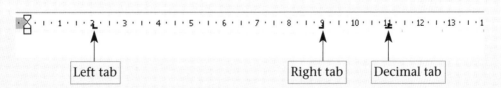

Figure 5.4 Using different tabs

1   Open a new file.
2   Key in the heading **Pool Charges** and press Enter twice.
3   Select a left tab ⌊L⌋ (Figure 5.1) and click on 2 cm on the ruler to set a tab (Figure 5.4).

4   Select a right tab ⌐ and click on ruler at 9 cm.

5   Select a decimal tab ⊥ and click on ruler at 11 cm.

6   Press the Tab key – key in **Children**.

7   Press the Tab key – key in **Weekend**.

8   Press the Tab key – key in **£2.00**.

9   Press **Enter** to start a new line.

10   Repeat steps 6–9 to complete the table as follows:

Children	Weekend	£2.00
Adults	Monday–Friday	£2.75
Adults	Weekend	£3.50
Seniors	Monday–Friday	£1.95
Senior	Weekend	£2.25
Family	Weekly Pass	£10.50

Notice how the text and decimals line up.

11   Centre and embolden the heading

12   Save the file as **Pool Charges** into Section 5 folder.

13   Spellcheck and proofread. Resave if necessary.

14   Print.

Task 5.3   Changing tab settings

Drag tab marker

Vertical line

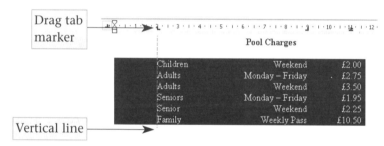

Figure 5.5 Changing tab settings

Method

1   Highlight all lines *of the table only*.

2   Position mouse pointer over the tab marker on the ruler at 2 cm.

3   Holding down the left mouse button, drag the tab marker to 1 cm. Notice the vertical line that appears to assist (Figure 5.5).

4   Drag the tab marker set at 9 cm to 8.5 cm.

5   Drag the tab marker set at 11 cm to 13 cm.

6   Click off the highlighted text to cancel highlighting.

7   Save the file as **Pool Charges 2** into Section 5 folder.

8   Print and close.

Information

To remove a tab, highlight the text from which the tab is to be removed, click on the tab marker in the ruler and drag downwards.

To set tabs using precise measurements, select **Tabs** from the **Format** menu.

> **Information:** Tables
>
> A table is a grid arrangement made up of a series of boxes called cells. They are also used for setting out text in columns and can be useful for creating simple forms. When working with tables it is usual to move across the rows, not down the columns. To move across a table press the Tab key. Text will automatically wrap onto the next line within a cell.

Task 5.4 Using the Table feature

The list of options on a menu changes to include those you have recently selected.

Method

1 Open a new file.
2 Switch to **Print Layout view** if not already displayed.
3 Key in a heading **Pool Opening Hours**.
4 Select **Table** menu (wait a few seconds for the full list or click on ⥥ at bottom of menu) – select **Insert** (Figure 5.6).
5 A further side menu appears – select **Table**.
6 Insert Table dialogue box appears (Figure 5.7).

Figure 5.6 Table menu   **Figure 5.7** Insert table

7 Key in **3** for Number of columns.
8 Key in **7** for Number of rows. Click OK.
9 A table grid appears.

Move across the table when keying in, not down.

Day	Opening time	Closing time
Monday	7.30 am	9 pm
Tuesday	7.30 am	10 pm
Wednesday	7.30 am	10 pm
Thursday	7.30 am	10 pm
Friday	7.30 am	9 pm
Saturday	9 am	9 pm

10 In the first box, key in **Day**.
11 Press **Tab** key to move across to the next cell.
12 Key in **Opening time**.

13 Press **Tab** key to move across to the next cell.
14 Key in **Closing time**.
15 Press **Tab** key to move to the next cell in the following row.
16 Continue to complete the table as above, pressing Tab key to move to the next cell.
17 Embolden the heading and the first line of the table.
18 Save the file as **Pool Opening Times** in Section 5 folder.
19 Spellcheck and proofread (particularly checking times). Resave if necessary.
20 Close the file.

Information

Tables can also be created by clicking on the **Insert Table** button and dragging to select the number of rows and columns required (Figure 5.8).

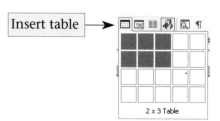

Figure 5.8 Using Insert Table button

Task 5.5 Inserting a new row

Sometimes you need to insert a new row inside the table or at the end.

Method

1 Open the file **Pool Opening Times** from Section 5 folder.
2 Position the cursor in the row below where the new row is required – in this case in the **Monday** row.
3 Select **Table** menu – **Insert** (Figure 5.9).
4 A side menu appears – select **Rows Above**.
5 Click into the last cell in the new row and key in **Last entry half an hour before closing time**. Notice how the text wraps onto the next line when necessary.
6 Position the cursor in the last cell at the bottom of the table after the text **9 pm**.
7 Press **Tab** key to create a new row.
8 Key in **Sunday** in the first cell, **9 am** and **9 pm** in the remaining two.
9 Spellcheck, proofread and save.

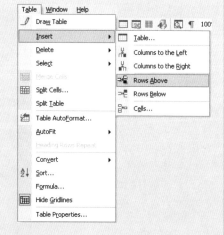

Figure 5.9 Insert a row

Information

New columns can also be inserted via **Insert** on the Table menu. Select Columns to the Left or Columns to the Right as required (Figure 5.9).

Task 5.6 — Changing column width and row height

Method

1 Open the file **Pool Opening Times** if not already open.
2 Position the mouse pointer on the **column** boundary line you want to move (in this case between the first and second) until it changes to +‖+ – you need to be quite precise (Figure 5.10).

Day	Opening time	Closing time
+‖+		Last entry half an hour before closing time
Monday	7.30 am	9 pm
Tuesday	7.30 am	10 pm
Wednesday	7.30 am	10 pm
Thursday	7.30 am	10 pm
Friday	7.30 am	9 pm
Saturday	9 am	9 pm

Figure 5.10 Change column width

3 Drag the boundary line to the left to make the column narrower.
4 Repeat for the next column boundary.
5 Position the mouse pointer on the **row** boundary you want to move (in this case below the heading **Day**) until it changes to a ‡.
6 Drag the boundary line down a little to increase the row height.
7 Save the file.

Information

Columns and rows can be given specific heights by highlighting the row (click to the left of the row), or column (click just above the column) and selecting **Table properties** from the Table menu. You may find this easier.

Task 5.7 — Deleting a row (or column)

Method

1 Position the cursor within the row or column to be deleted (in this case the second row with the blank cells).
2 Select the **Table** menu and select **Delete**.
3 A side menu appears – select **Rows** (or **Columns** if required).
4 Reduce the width of the last column to balance the look of the table by dragging the right-hand boundary line towards the left.
5 Save and print.

Task 5.8 — Removing the table borders

Method

1 Highlight the table by positioning the mouse pointer in the left margin alongside the first line of the table. The mouse pointer changes to an arrow pointing right.

2 Hold down the left mouse button and drag down to the bottom row of the table (Figure 5.11).

Day	Opening Times	Closing Time
Monday	7.30 am	9 pm
Tuesday	7.30 am	10 pm
Wednesday	7.30 am	10 pm
Thursday	7.30 am	10 pm
Friday	7.30 am	9 pm
Saturday	9 am	9pm
Sunday	9 am	9 pm

Figure 5.11 Select table

3 Click on the down arrow by the **Border** button (Figure 5.12).

4 Click on the **No Border** button. Click off highlighted area to remove highlighting. Whilst the border now appears grey onscreen, this will not print.

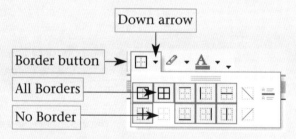

Figure 5.12 Table Borders

5 Save and print.

To add borders to a table without any, highlight table and click on **All Borders**.

Information

Tables are useful not only for lists, but for a variety of documents such as forms.

Information: Bullets and numbering

- **Bullets** are used to give emphasis to a list of items – as in the list of the topics at the beginning of each section of this book.
- **Numbering** is used to automatically number a list of items.

  Both can be applied before or after keying in a list.

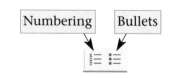

Figure 5.13 Bullets and numbering

Task 5.9 — Create lists using numbers and bullets

Method

1. Open a new file and key in **List of current destinations**.
2. Press **Enter** twice.
3. Click on the Numbering button (Figure 5.13) and key in **Spain**. (Numbers are indented from the margin by default.)
4. Press **Enter** and key in **France**.
5. Press **Enter** and key in **Portugal**.
6. Press **Enter** and key in **Holland**.
7. Press **Enter** twice. Notice how the numbering stops.
8. Key in the heading **New destinations**.
9. Press Enter twice.
10. Click on the **Bullets** button and key in **Germany**.
11. Press **Enter** and key in **Luxembourg**.
12. Press **Enter** and key in **Italy**.
13. Press **Enter** twice. Notice how the bullets stop.

Save your work every 10 minutes.

Task 5.10 — Remove and reapply numbers and bullets

Method

1. Highlight the numbered words. Note the numbers themselves are not highlighted.
2. Click on the **Numbering** button to remove.
3. Highlight the bulleted items.
4. Click on the **Bullets** button to remove.
5. Highlight the first four countries.
6. Click on the **Bullets** button.
7. Highlight the last three countries.
8. Click on the **Numbering** button.

Note:

To avoid backache when working at your computer, make sure your chair is adjusted properly to support your back.

Information

A numbered list can be changed directly to bullets by highlighting and then clicking on the **Bullets** button, and vice versa.

This method of indenting can be used for any type of paragraph.

Hint:

If numbering goes wrong, highlight the items in the list and click on the **Numbering** button to remove numbers. Adjust the text if necessary, highlight the list and click back on the **Numbering** button.

Method

1 Highlight the numbered words.
2 Select **Paragraph** from the **Format** menu.
3 Select **Indents and Spacing** tab.
4 Key in **3** in the **Left Indentation** box.
5 Click on **OK**.
6 Close the file without saving.

Indents and spacing

Left Indent

Paragraph

Indents and Spacing | Line and Page Breaks

General
Alignment: [Left ▼]   Outline

Indentation
Left: [3]   Specia
Right: [0 cm]   Hangi

Figure 5.14 Indent

→ Practise your skills 1

1 Open a new file and set tabs as follows:
Right tab at 3 cm | Left tab at 4 cm | Centre tab at 9 cm

2 Key in the following text:

UK BRANCH OFFICES

Branch	Manager	Number of staff
Belfast	Brendan Carson	24
Birmingham	Ping Zhiyuan	23
Cardiff	Rhiannon Lloyd	21
Edinburgh	Daniel Blythe	26
London	Bridget Murphy	32
Manchester	Colin Day	19
Oxford	Kari Costello	18

NEW OFFICES PLANNED:

Manchester
Liverpool
Brighton

Note:

Make sure you are in **My Documents** before creating the new folder. **Save in:** box should read My Documents. If not, click on My Documents in side bar of Save dialogue box (see Figure 4.2 in Section 4).

3 Spellcheck and proofread, particularly checking names and numbers.
4 Make the list of new offices a numbered list.
5 Embolden the main heading and increase the font size to 16.
6 Embolden the column headings and underline each one separately.
7 Embolden the NEW OFFICES PLANNED heading and change to font size 14.
8 Save as **UK Branch Offices** into a new folder called **Skills Practice**.

9 Print.

10 Change the numbered list to bullets and change the indent to 6 cm.

11 Alter the tab settings for the list of branches as follows:
Move tab at 9 cm to 11 cm | tab at 4 cm to 6 cm | tab at 3 cm to 4 cm.

12 Centre the main heading and NEW OFFICES PLANNED.

13 Save as **Branches 2**.

14 Use **Save As** to save the file using the same name to floppy disk.

15 Print 2 copies and close.

Hint:

Don't forget to highlight all rows first.

→ Practise your skills 2

1 Open a new file.

2 Key in the heading **CRAFT COURSES COMING SOON!** Press **Enter** twice.

3 Key in the following text:

We hope you are enjoying your current course. Next term we are hoping to offer the courses listed below. If you are interested in any of these, please tick in the appropriate box and return to your tutor. We will then send you further details.

4 Press Enter twice.

5 Insert a table 3 columns wide, 7 rows deep, and key in the text below:

Course title	Content	Tick here
Silk painting	Learn to produce the wonderful effects that can be achieved by paint on silk	
Pottery	Have a go at throwing your own pots!	
Ceramics	Produce your very own creations using this medium	
Creative collage	Build up unique works of art using fabrics and other materials	
Working with stained glass	Create a glass panel to your own design using coloured and textured glass	
Mosaics	Use a variety of materials – tiles, old crockery, mirrors etc – to stunning effect	

6 Position the cursor below the table, press Enter once.

7 Insert a two column, one row table and key in as follows:

Your name	

8 Increase the height of the row as above.

9 Centre and embolden the main heading increasing font size to 24.

10 Embolden the headings in the first row.

11 Change the font of the whole document to a font of your choice.

12 Spellcheck and proofread.

13 Save as **Craft Courses** into **Skills Practice** folder and print.

14 Increase the width of the second column.

15 Increase the height of the first row.

16 Insert a row after the first row – leave this blank.

17 Delete the Ceramics row.

18 Save as **Craft Courses 2**.

19 Use **Save As** to save the file using the same name to floppy disk.

20 Print and close.

→ Check your knowledge

Identify the following tab markers:

1 ⊥

2 ⊥

3 ⌐

4 L

5 How can you delete a tab setting from a paragraph?

6 When keying in text, how do you move to the next tab setting?

7 How can you change a numbered list into bullets?

8 How can you change the width of a column in a table?

9 What is this toolbar button used for? ⊞

10 When printing a table how can you prevent the borders from printing?

Section 6   Page formatting and layout

You will learn to

- Select paper size and orientation
- Work in different page views
- Set margin settings
- Indent paragraphs
- Change line spacing
- Insert page breaks
- Create headers and footers
- Number pages

In this section you will learn about paper sizes and how you would set out pages on the different sizes and orientations of paper.

Information: Paper size

So far you have probably only worked with paper of one size – the standard size used for printers and photocopiers, which is **A4** (the size of pages in this book). This is based on (ISO) International Standard sizes, where each size is half that of the next biggest size.

A3	A4	A5	A6
297 × 420 mm	210 × 297 mm	148 × 210 mm	105 × 148 mm

Generally, all printers take A4 paper and most will handle smaller sizes. Those that accept A3 paper are less common and anything bigger than A3 would require specialist printing.

Typical uses

A3   Drawings, diagrams, posters
A4   Letters, memos, advertising flyers, forms, reports, booklets, newsletters
A5   Memos, advertising flyers, booklets, forms, notepads
A6   Postcards, invitations, notepads, advertisements

Page orientation

Short edge at the top

Short edge at the side

Portrait   Landscape

A page can be set up as either portrait (tall) or landscape (wide). Most documents on A4 will use portrait orientation.

Method

Hint:

Letter, Legal and Executive are American/Canadian paper sizes.

1   Open the file **European Currency 2** from My Documents.
2   Change the font size throughout to size **12**.
3   Split the first paragraph so the new one starts with **The euro symbol** . . .
4   Select **Page Setup** from the **File** menu and click on the **Paper** tab (Figure 6.1).

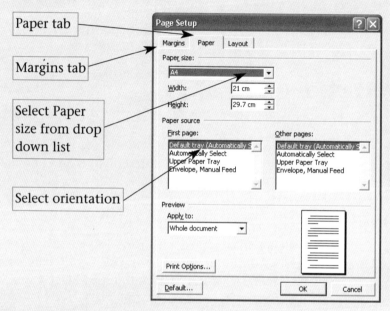

Figure 6.1 Paper size and orientation

5   Select **A5** from the drop down list.
6   Click on the **Margins** and check **Portrait** orientation is selected.
7   Click **OK**.

Hint:

To remember which is which paper orientation, think of a wide scenic view for landscape and a tall portrait painting for portrait.

Remember:

A soft copy is what you see on screen. A hard copy is a printout.

Information: Page views

So far you have probably worked in **Normal View**, which allows you to enter and edit text quickly, simplifying the page layout, e.g. graphics and images do not display.

Print Layout View lets you see how text and graphics will be positioned on the printed page. This is a called a **WYSIWYG** display – **W**hat **Y**ou **S**ee **I**s **W**hat **Y**ou **G**et. In other words, what you see on the screen is what will appear on your hard copy – the printout. It can be useful to see, as you are working, what the finished page will look like and many people prefer to work using this view.

Print Preview allows you to preview the whole page as it will print in various magnifications, and gives you a chance to adjust features such as margins and font size to suit. It is possible to preview multiple pages, which is very useful for checking the appearance of a long document to ensure consistency and a pleasing layout, and to fine-tune page breaks. Other elements such as graphics can be repositioned to achieve balance.

Method

I   Click on the **Print Layout View** button – bottom left of document window (Figure 6.2). Notice how you can see the top and sides of the page.

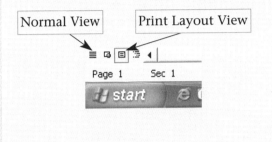

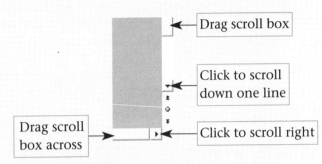

Figure 6.2 Page views

Figure 6.3 Scroll bars

2   Use the scroll bars to scroll down to see the bottom and back up to the top (Figure 6.3).

3   Click on the **Print Preview** button ⬚ in the **Standard toolbar** (Figure 6.4).

Figure 6.4 Print Preview

Preview opens. The mouse pointer changes to a magnifying glass when positioned over the selected page area. Click on the page to zoom in and click again to zoom out.

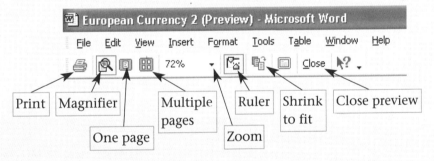

Figure 6.5 Preview toolbar

4   Click on the down arrow beside **Zoom** and select **50%.** Try other Zoom settings.

5   Click on view **One page** button.

6   Use **Save As** to save the file as **The Euro A5** into a new folder called **Section 6**. Leave the file open.

NOTE: Make sure the **Save in:** box reads **My Documents** before creating the new folder.

Hint:

You must use the File menu to save in Print Preview.

Task 6.3   Editing in Page Preview mode

Method

1   Click on the **Magnifier** 🔍 button. As the mouse pointer is moved onto the page it changes to an 'I-beam' to allow editing.

2   Notice how the status bar at the bottom left of the document window shows there are two pages (Figure 6.6).

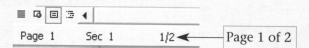

Figure 6.6 Two-page document

3   Click on the **Multiple Pages** 🔳 button and drag across the first two 'pages' to view pages side by side (Figure 6.7).

4   Click on **Shrink to Fit** 📑 (Figure 6.5).

This is most useful for fitting a document onto one page if a few lines of text spill over onto a second page, by reducing the size of the text.

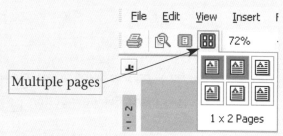

Figure 6.7 View multiple pages

Information: Page margins

The width of margins can be varied according to the requirements of the document. If you had to produce a letter to be printed on headed paper for example, you might have to leave a wider margin at the top of the page to accommodate the company logo and other details. You may want to reduce or increase the margins of a document to improve the overall layout, e.g. a notice or advertisement. As a general rule, the right margin should not normally be wider than the left although they may be equal, and the top margin should not be bigger than the bottom, as the page can look top heavy and unbalanced. Margins for smaller paper sizes, e.g. A5, are usually smaller than for A4.

Task 6.4   Change margins using rulers

This can be carried out in Print Preview or Print Layout View.

Method

1   In **Print Preview** mode, click on the **View Ruler** button 🖳 (Figure 6.5) to display the horizontal and vertical rulers if they are not already present. (The rulers are already displayed in Print Layout View.)

2   Position mouse pointer on the top vertical margin boundary (Figure 6.8) and when it changes to a double-headed arrow ↕, drag the margin boundary up slightly. Repeat with the bottom margin boundary.

Figure 6.8 Change margin using vertical ruler

3   Position mouse pointer on the horizontal margin boundary
    (Figure 6.9) and when it changes to a double-headed arrow ↔,
    drag the margin boundary to the left slightly. **Note**: This can be
    tricky and you might move the left indent to the right out of
    the way first. *Don't forget to move it back.*

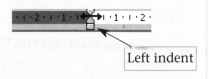

Left indent

4   Drag the right margin boundary slightly to the right.

Figure 6.9 Change margin using horizontal ruler

5   Close Print Preview (Figure 6.5) and return to Print Layout View.
6   Load your printer with A5 paper. Check with your printer manual or your tutor how to do this (all
    printers are different). If you do not have access to A5, print on A4.
7   Save the file.

Information

Margins can also be changed in Print Preview or Print Layout View using the rulers. This is useful for
making adjustments to a document prior to printing, which you may be required to do.

| Task 6.5 | Change margin settings using the File menu |

Method

I   Select **Page Setup** from the **File** menu. Click on the **Margins** tab (Figure 6.10).

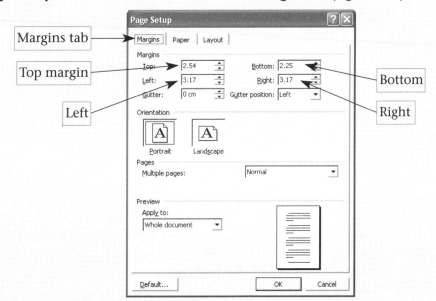

Figure 6.10 Margins showing default settings

2   Click into the **Top** margin box, delete the current setting and key in 2.75.
3   Press Tab key to move into **Bottom** margin box, delete the current setting and key in 2.75.
    Repeat for **Left** and **Right** margins. Click **OK**.
4   Save and close the file.

Information: Paragraph format

Documents are divided into paragraphs, forming natural pauses or breaks, usually where a new idea or topic is raised. A whole page of continuous text is difficult to read and the use of paragraphs can improve the visual appearance of a document. Sometimes a paragraph needs to stand out from the rest of a document and, depending on its purpose, may be given a heading or subheading. Another method is to indent, or set in from the margins, on the left or both sides. This should not be confused, however, with changing margins.

| Task 6.6 | Indent from the left using the toolbar |

Method

1   Open the file **The Euro A5** from Section 6 folder in **Print Layout View**.
2   Split the first paragraph to make the new paragraph begin **The euro symbol ...**
3   Position cursor inside the new paragraph.
4   Click on **Increase indent** to move the paragraph in by one tab stop (Figure 6.11).

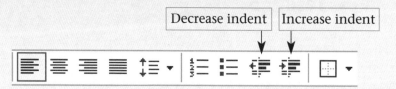

Figure 6.11 Indent

5   Click on **Decrease indent** to move the paragraph back again.

| Task 6.7 | Indent on both sides of a paragraph |

You have already used this method for indenting bullets and numbering by a specified amount.

Method

1   Position cursor in the second paragraph.
2   Select **Paragraph** from the **Format** menu (Figure 6.12).
3   Select **Indents and Spacing** tab.
4   Key in **1** in the **Left** box.
5   Key in **1** in the **Right** box.
6   Click on **OK**.
7   Save the file.

Hint:

You do not need to key in cm – just the number is enough.

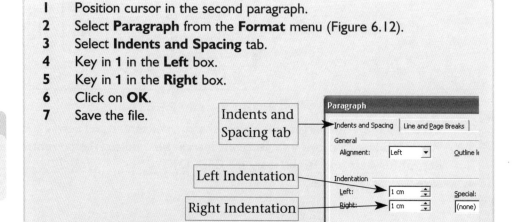

Figure 6.12 Indent left and right

Information

To indent several paragraphs together using either method, you must highlight them all first.

Information: Line spacing

Line spacing determines the amount of space between lines of text. Single spacing is the default. Double spacing is often used for draft copies of documents. Spacing can easily be changed by either positioning the cursor inside a paragraph or highlighting several paragraphs together or even the entire document (**Edit** menu – **Select All**), and then using keyboard shortcuts known as **hot keys**.

Single	**Control + 1**	the default setting
Double	**Control + 2**	leaves one clear line space between lines, often used for draft documents
1.5	**Control + 5**	leaves one-and-a-half line space between lines

Task 6.8 | Change line spacing

Hint:

Line spacing and paragraph indents can also be applied by selecting **Paragraph** from the **Format** menu – **Indents and Spacing** tab.

Method

1. Position cursor in the second paragraph.
2. Press **Ctrl + 2** for double line spacing (hold down Control key and press 2).
3. Press **Ctrl + 1** for single line spacing.
4. Press **Ctrl + 5** for 1.5 line spacing.
5. Save the file.

Information: Working with multiple pages

When dealing with multi-page documents it is important to avoid **widow and orphan lines**. These are single lines that appear at the top or bottom of a page separated from the rest of the paragraph. Ensure that **Widow/Orphan control** box is ticked. See the **Format** menu – **Paragraph** option – **Line and Page Breaks** tab (Figure 6.13).

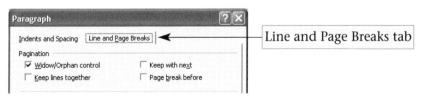

Figure 6.13 Window/Orphan control

When text reaches the bottom margin, Word automatically inserts a page break and starts a new page – this is called a **soft page break**. If you edit the document by inserting or deleting sections of text, this will automatically be repositioned. If you manually insert a page break, its position remains fixed whatever editing takes place. This is called a **hard page break**.

Task 6.9 — Insert a hard page break

Method

1 Open the file **The Euro A5** from Section 6 folder if not already open.
2 Make sure you are in **Print Layout View** (Figure 6.2).
3 Key in the following text as a new paragraph after the paragraph ending ...**feature of that nation**.

> Euro notes are identical. The notes are in denominations of €500, €200, €100, €50, €20, €10 and €5. These can be used anywhere within the euro area, regardless of country of issue. The notes have a number of security features such as watermarks on both sides and a security thread. The notes are printed in raised ink to give a distinctive feel and each note features a hologram showing the value of the note and the euro symbol.

4 Notice how the page breaks as you reach the bottom margin.
5 Key in the following text as a new final paragraph.

> The coins are in denominations of €2, €1, 50 cent, 20 cent, 10 cent, 5 cent, 2 cent and 1 cent. There are 100 cents to €1. The common European face of the coins represents a map of the European Union against a background of lines to which are attached the stars of the European flag.

6 Position the cursor in front of the paragraph that starts **To help the blind ...**
7 Select **Break** from the **Insert** menu.
8 Click on **Page break** and click **OK**.
9 Change to **Normal View** (Figure 6.2) and move through the document using the scroll bar (or Page Up/Down keys) to see where the soft page break appears as a dotted line. The hard break appears as a dotted line with the words **Page break** in the middle.

Remember:

For the euro symbol €, press Alt Gr + 4.

Remember:

A page break that occurs naturally is a **soft page break**.

Task 6.10 — Delete a page break

Method

1 In **Normal** View, position the cursor on the hard page break you inserted and press **Delete**. (**Note**: you cannot delete a soft page break.)
2 Switch back to **Print Layout View** (Figure 6.2).
3 Save the file.

Information: Headers, Footers and Page Numbers

A **header** or a **footer** is a piece of text that appears at the top or bottom of every page throughout a document, for example the name of the document. It is also where page numbers are placed. It is always wise to number multiple pages so the reader can follow the sequence in a logical order. If papers become mixed up, the numbering means they can be easily reassembled. Page numbers also serve as a reference point, e.g. 'see page 10'. As well as simple numbering, a page total can be included, e.g. Page 3 of 5, so the reader knows the total number of pages they should have and whether or not the document is complete. Page numbers can be placed within the margin at the top of the page (in the **header**) or, more usually, at the bottom (in the **footer**). Headers and footers can only be seen in **Print Layout View**. Ensure this is selected.

Remember

Anything placed in the header appears at the top of every page of a document, and if placed in the footer, at the bottom.

Task 6.11 Add a header and number pages in a footer

Method

1 Select **Header and Footer** from the **View** menu. Notice how the document text is 'greyed out' and a header box appears with the cursor flashing inside. Key in your name.

2 Click on **Switch between Header and Footer** 📑 to move to the footer (Figure 6.14).

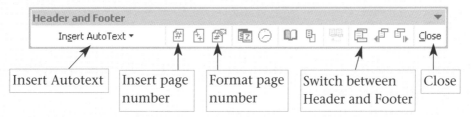

Figure 6.14 Header/Footer

3 Click on **Insert Page Number** 🔢 and click on the **Centre** button ≡ on the formatting toolbar.

4 Click on **Close**.

Task 6.12 Start numbering at a number other than 1

If the document you are working on is one of several which will eventually form a longer document, you may not want numbering to start at page one.

Method

1 Select **Header and Footer** from the **View** menu and click on **Switch between Header and Footer** 🔛 to move to the footer.

2 Click on **Format Page Number** 🔢 (Figure 6.14).

3 Click in **Start at:** and key in **3** in the box alongside (Figure 6.15).

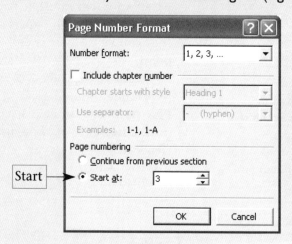

Start →

Figure 6.15 Page Number Format

4 Click **OK**.

5 Close the Header and Footer toolbar. Check to see the result.

6 Now change numbering back to start at 1.

Note:

Another reason for not starting numbering at page 1 is if there is a front cover or contents page which should not be numbered.

Task 6.13	Number pages including page totals

Method

1 Select **Header and Footer** from the **View** menu and click on **Switch between Header and Footer** 🔛 to move to the footer.

2 Delete the existing page number and click on **Insert AutoText** (Figure 6.14) and select **Page X of Y**.

3 Click on **Align right** button on the formatting toolbar.

4 Click on **Close** to close the Header and Footer toolbar.

5 Save and print the file on A5. Close the file.

Remember:

Choose **Select All** from the **Edit** menu to select entire documents.

Information

A single page number can also be inserted using **Page Numbers** from the **Insert** menu.

To delete page numbers select **Header and Footer** from the **View** menu, switch to footer if required, highlight the number/s and delete.

→ Practise your skills 1

1 Open the file **The Euro A5** from the **Section 6** folder.
2 Change the page size to A4.
3 Remove the indent from the second paragraph.
4 Indent both the paragraphs that list the different denominations (values) of coins and notes, by 1 cm on each side.
5 Change the line spacing for the entire document to double.
6 Change the font size for the whole document to size 12.
7 Increase the heading to size 16.
8 Delete existing page totals and insert simple page numbers starting at 4.
9 Insert a page break in front of **Euro notes are identical ...**
10 Save as **Draft Euro Currency** onto floppy disk.
11 Print and close.

→ Practise your skills 2

1 Open the file **Draft Euro Currency** from floppy disk.
2 Remove the hard page break.
3 Start page numbering at page 1.
4 Remove the indent from any paragraph that is formatted this way.
5 Change line spacing to 1.5.
6 Change all margins to 3 cm.
7 Check layout in Print Preview.
8 Make sure the document fits onto one page.
9 Save as **Final Draft Euro Currency** to **Section 6** folder.
10 Print 2 copies.

Remember

Shrink to fit can be used when several lines spill onto a second page.

→ Check your knowledge

1 What paper size and orientation are the pages of this book?
2 What is WYSIWYG?
3 What is the importance of checking document layout using WYSIWYG?
4 What are typical uses for A4 paper?
5 What general rule should you follow when setting margins?
6 What is Shrink to Fit?
7 Name one way of indenting paragraphs.
8 What is the difference between a hard and soft page break?
9 What is widow/orphan control?
10 Why is it important to number pages and why include a page total?

Consolidation 2

Information

An **agenda** is a document distributed before a meeting that informs people of the date, time and place of a meeting, together with a list of items to be discussed and the order in which they will be dealt with. **Minutes** are a record of what was discussed at a meeting, detailing any action to be taken and by whom. These would be distributed following a meeting.

Task 1

1 Key in the following agenda on A5 portrait paper. Format headings etc as you feel fit. Save the file as **Agenda 2 Sept** into a new folder called **Consolidation**. Spellcheck and proofread. Print the file on A5.

Tilbury Staff Social Club
Meeting to be held in Meeting Room 3
On 2 September at 12.30 pm

Agenda

1 Apologies
2 Minutes of last meeting
3 Matters arising
4 Day trip to France
5 Quiz Evening
6 Any other business
7 Date and time of next meeting

Task 2

Using the same file as above:
1 Change the page setup to A4 portrait.
2 Set the margins on 3 cm all round.
3 Change the line spacing for the numbered list to double.
4 Indent the numbered list to 5 cm.
5 Centre all the headings above the agenda list.
6 Insert a page break following the agenda.
7 Number the pages showing the page total and align to the right.
8 Key in the minutes below, formatting appropriately.
9 Spellcheck and proofread.
10 Use Save As to save the file as **Agenda and Minutes 2 Sept** into the Consolidation folder.
11 Use Save As to save the file to floppy disk and print.

Tilbury Staff Social Club
Minutes of the meeting held on Monday 2 September

Present:
Finn Burton
Gill Hunt
Nia Jones
Jonathan Lee
Nasir Mahmood
Joanne Price

Item		Action
Apologies	Dave Brown sent his apologies.	
Minutes of last meeting	Minutes were accepted as a true record of the meeting.	
Matters arising	There were none.	
Day trip to France	Thirty-nine people had signed up and the tickets and coach would now be booked.	JP
Quiz Evening	It was decided to go ahead with this event sometime before Christmas, date to be arranged. Gill Hunt agreed to be question master and will start researching questions nearer the time. Nasir Mahmood suggested that management might be asked to contribute wine for the evening. He agreed to approach the MD.	GH NM
Any other business	Finn Burton suggested a theatre trip in the New Year. He agreed to find out what might be suitable.	FB
Date and time of next meeting	To be circulated later.	JP

Section 7 | Inserting graphics

You will learn to

- Insert and manipulate clip art
- Insert WordArt
- Consider how to position graphics
- Insert symbols

In this section you will find out how to insert images and other graphical features into your documents.

Hint:

You can turn toolbars on and off by selecting **Toolbars** from the **View** menu.

To insert graphics you need the **Drawing toolbar**. To show this, click on the Drawing button (Figure 7.1). The toolbar appears at the bottom of the screen (Figure 7.2).

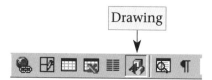

Figure 7.1 Drawing button

The Drawing toolbar offers a variety of graphical features that you may want to experiment with, but this section deals with clip art and WordArt.

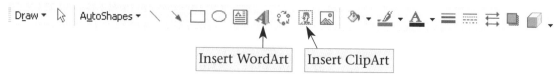

Figure 7.2 Drawing toolbar

Information

Word has a collection of clip art images. You can search the collection for an image that matches a descriptive key word.

Task 7.1 | Insert, resize and move clip art

Method

1 Open a new file. Ensure you are working in Print Layout View.
2 Click on 🖼 **Insert ClipArt** from the Drawing toolbar (Figure 7.2). The **Insert Clip Art** task pane appears on the right-hand side of the window (Figure 7.3).

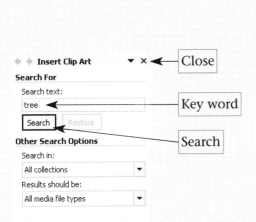

Figure 7.3 Insert clip art

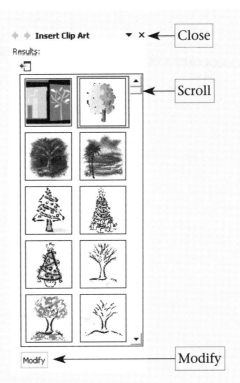

Figure 7.4 Select clip art

3   Click in the **Search text:** box and type in a word to find a picture of your choice e.g. **tree**.
4   Click on **Search**. Clip art images appear (Figure 7.4).
5   View the images by scrolling down and click on any one to insert it onto the page.
6   The image appears – click on it and selection handles appear around the edges (Figure 7.5).
7   Position pointer over a corner handle – pointer changes to diagonal double-headed arrow – and drag inwards towards the middle of the image to make it smaller.

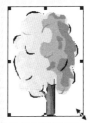

Figure 7.5 Resize image

Note: Always resize using a *corner* handle to keep the image in proportion.

At this stage the image cannot be moved freely on the page as it is embedded in the text line and will move with any text. Text wrap needs to be applied to separate and free it.

8   If not already selected, click on the image. The Picture toolbar should appear (Figure 7.6). If not, select **Toolbars** from the **View** menu and then select **Picture**.

Figure 7.6 Picture toolbar

9   Click on **Text wrapping** button and select **Square**. (The handles change in appearance.) This would cause any text to wrap around the image in a square shape.
10 Position pointer over image – it changes to a four-headed arrow. Hold down the mouse button and drag the image to a new position.

Task 7.2 — Modify a search

Hint:

Clip art can also be selected using the following options seen at the bottom of the Insert Clip Art Task pane:

Clip Organizer

Clips Online

Method

1. Click on **Modify** (Figure 7.4).
2. Key in a new search word e.g. **flower** and click on **Search**.
3. View the images by scrolling down and click on any one to add to your publication.
4. Apply **Square** text wrapping.
5. Repeat this several times using different search words of your choice.
6. Arrange the clip art images on the page.
7. Save the file as **Clip art** into a new Section 7 folder.
8. Close the Clip Art task pane by clicking on ✖ . (See Figure 7.4)

Task 7.3 — Resize clip art to a specific size

Method

1. Click on image to select it.
2. Choose **Picture** from the **Format** menu.
3. Select **Size** tab (Figure 7.7).

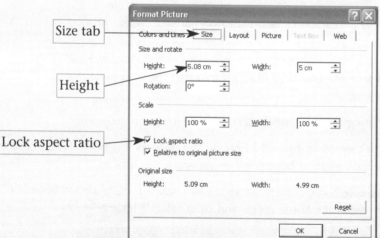

Figure 7.7 Resize clip art

4. Ensure **Lock aspect ratio** is checked on – check box should be ticked. This will ensure the image stays in proportion and is not distorted.
5. In height box, delete measurement and key in 4.
6. Click **OK**.

Information: Copy and paste

Copying an image allows you to place a copy of the image elsewhere in the document whilst keeping the original in place. When you copy an image, the copy is held in an area of memory called the **clipboard**, ready to paste into the document. (This feature also works with text and other objects.)

Task 7.4 — Copy and paste an image

Method

1 Open the file **Curtains and Blinds** created in Section 3 and stored in My Documents.
2 Insert clip art searching on the word **curtain** or **window**.
3 Apply the text wrap option **In front of text**. (This allows an image to sit on a layer on top of a text layer without moving the text away.)
4 With the image selected, click on the **Copy** button on the Standard toolbar (Figure 7.8).
5 Click on **Paste**. A copy appears on top of the original.
6 Position pointer over graphic and drag to move it to the opposite side of the page.
7 Save the file.

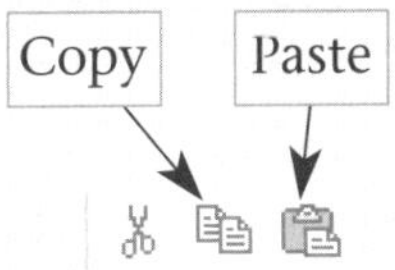

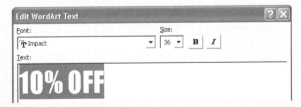

Figure 7.8 Copy and paste

Information: WordArt

WordArt is fancy text that is placed on the page as a graphical object (like an image) and can be moved around the page independently and resized as required.

Task 7.5 — Insert WordArt

Method

1 Click on the **Insert WordArt** button 📐 on the Drawing toolbar.
2 Choose one of the WordArt styles and click on **OK**.
3 Key in the text required **10% OFF** (Figure 7.9). Notice that the font and size can be altered if required. Click on OK.

Edit WordArt Text
Font: Impact   Size: 36   **B** *I*
Text:
10% OFF

Figure 7.9 WordArt text

4 Select the WordArt and apply text wrapping as before. Position pointer over the WordArt – it changes to a four-headed arrow. Hold down the mouse button and drag the WordArt to a new position at the bottom of the page.

5 Resize if required by dragging a corner handle inwards or outwards.
6 Reshape it by dragging any other handle inwards or outwards.
   (WordArt does not have to be kept in proportion like clip art.)
7 Save the file, print and close.

Information: Consider how to position graphics

When using images with solid blocks of text, you must always consider readability. Experiment with the position of the image in the following task to help decide a suitable place for it. Never put it in the middle with text wrapping on all sides. This can cause the reader to lose their place when their eyes have to jump over the image to read the remainder of a line. When text spreads across the page from margin to margin, always put the image somewhere around the edge, so the text wraps on three or less sides. Remember, graphics should enhance a document, not get in the way.

Hint:

Do not clutter your pages with graphics. Use them sparingly.

Hint:

Images that are embedded or in line with text can be seen in either Print Layout View or Normal View. Images with text wrap applied are not visible in Normal View. Neither is WordArt or drawing objects.

Remember:

Graphics should not get in the way of the text.

Task 7.6 — Use text wrap with continuous text

Method

The following instruction will automatically insert text onto the page.
1 Key in =**rand(10)** and press **Enter**.
2 Insert a clip art image and click on it to select.
3 Click on the **Text wrapping** button as before, and select **Square**.
4 Move the image into various positions to decide on a suitable position.
5 Experiment with the other text wrapping options to see their effect.
6 Close the file without saving.

Information: Choosing text wrap

There are several text wrap options to choose from, but safe choices are:

• For solid blocks of text, choose **square** text wrap so the text moves away from the image.
• For display text, e.g. advertisements, use **in Front of Text**, so the text position is not affected by the image.

Information: Symbols

Symbols are small graphical images that are part of a font's character set. Different fonts have different symbols. The following are examples of the font Wingdings' symbols:

↖ ✎ ✂ 📖 ⊠ ✓

As they are in fact text characters, they can be made bigger or smaller in the same way as ordinary text – i.e. by highlighting and selecting a font size.

Task 7.7 — Insert symbols

Method

1 Open a new file.
2 Select **Symbol** from the **Insert** menu.
3 Select the font **Wingdings** from the drop down list (Figure 7.10).

Note:

These symbols are sometimes known as dingbats.

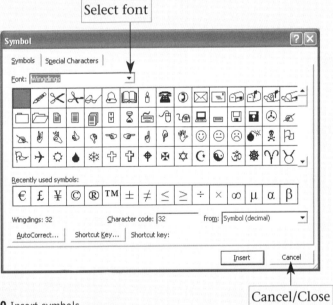

Figure 7.10 Insert symbols

4 Click on a symbol to select it.
5 Double click on a symbol to insert into the document.
6 Insert several different symbols.
7 Close the Symbol dialogue box.
8 Change the size of the symbols.
9 Repeat the task trying different fonts.
10 Close the file without saving.

→ Practise your skills 1

1 Open the file **Foremans advert 3** created in Section 3.
2 Change the document setup to A5 landscape.
3 Insert a suitable piece of clip art and resize it to a width of 2 cm ensuring aspect ratio (proportion) is maintained.
4 Set text wrapping to **In front of text** and move to a suitable position.
5 Copy the image and place in suitable position.
6 Insert WordArt saying **Sale**. Resize if necessary.
7 Copy it and place both in suitable positions.
8 Below the address, key in the following: ☎ 0191 768452 (symbol from Wingdings 2).
9 Print preview the page and adjust images if necessary.
10 Adjust margins to balance the advertisement on the page.
11 Save as **Foremans advert final** into the Skills Practice folder and print.

→ Practise your skills 2

1 Open the file Feng Shui saved in My Documents.
2 Change the page setup to A5 landscape with margins of 3 cm all round.
3 Format appropriately, choosing font size etc.
4 Search for two pieces of clip art – wind, water or China – and position. Use square text wrap.
5 Proofread carefully, checking spelling and layout.
6 Save as **Feng Shui 3** into the Skills Practice folder and print.
7 Change page setup to A5 portrait.
8 Adjust layout and formatting as necessary.
9 Change alignment to justified.
10 Save as **Feng Shui 4** into the Skills Practice folder and print.

> **Hint:**
>
> Alternative search words could be house, furniture or nature. You could also try Clip Organizer or Clips Online.

→ Check your knowledge

1 How can you ensure an image stays in proportion when resizing?
2 How can the use and positioning of graphics improve a document's appearance?
3 What is the purpose of locking aspect ratio?
4 What is applied to an image to make it possible to move it anywhere on the page?
5 Why would you not put an image in the middle of a page of solid text?

Section 8   Proofreading

You will learn to

- Understand the importance of proofreading and accuracy
- Proofread your work

Proofreading involves checking the text to make sure it follows the house style, and that the meaning, grammar, spelling and information are accurate. It also involves checking the alignment of text, the position of the graphics, and how easy the text is to read.

Information: Proofreading

Very often in business, the only communication an organisation has with its clients or customers is by correspondence or its documents. Any impression that might be formed may be that given by the documents only, and therefore they stand to represent that organisation. It is no different when creating documents for yourself. If, for example, you are applying for a job, you naturally want to give the best impression you can.

When working from original documents it is obviously vital that you copy carefully. You must copy names accurately to avoid offending or annoying the recipient, or, at the very least, appearing careless. Ensure you reproduce any numbers correctly. A mistyped number could mean a wrong quantity is supplied and cost you or your organisation a fortune! A wrong telephone number could lose that all-important call. A wrong date could mean a lost meeting. A wrong amount of money could lose a contract. An error might cause a problem on a legal technicality, so the consequences of that typing error might be huge! Does the document convey the intended meaning?

Of course, use the spellcheck, but proofreading necessitates the careful visual checking of your document, not only for errors in the text but also the layout.

You should always:

- Check onscreen for misuse of words that the spellcheck has not picked up.
- Ensure the document conveys the meaning that was intended.
- Check carefully against the original text you may be working from.
- Check the correct forms of words have been used, e.g. their/there, border/boarder, where/were.
- Make sure that British English spellings are used and not American English.
- Check spelling of names, foreign words and any specialist/technical words.
- Check numbers to make sure they are correct and valid.
- Check any dates to make sure they are correct and valid – e.g. is it the right date, does the correct day match with the date?
- Check the layout carefully – is everything lined up properly, are images in the right position, is the text readable around graphics?
- Check for consistency in fonts and sizes – do they change in the middle of a document?
- Check graphics – are they in the right place, is the text readable around them?
- Check after making any amendments.
- Preview the page – does it look right?
- Check the document again after printing.
- Check with the originator of the document if applicable.

→ Practise your skills 1

Proofread the following text and note down the line number and word/s of any errors you spot where **B** differs from the original **A**. There are 12 errors to spot. Check your findings on page 84.

A	
1	The Norwegian holiday promised a cruise around fjords in and out around the
2	small islands and calling at picture-postcard fishing villages and deserted bays.
3	The scenery showed a marked contrast between the breathtaking mountains
4	and the little colourful villages. There was also the chance to make the never-
5	forgotten visit to the 'The Kingdom of the Whales' to see the magnificent
6	black and white orcas. All this – 7 days and 6 nights for only £475.

B	
1	The Norwegian holiday promised a cruise around fiords in and out around the
2	the small islands and calling at picture postcard fishing villages and deserted
3	bays. The scenery shows a market contrast between the breath-taking
4	mountains and the little colorful villages. There was also the chance to make
5	the never-forgotten visit to the 'The Kingdom for the Wales' to see
6	magnificent black and white orcas. All this – 7 days and nights for only £473.

→ Practise your skills 2

1 Read through the following and spot the errors. There are 10 in total – 7 words correctly spelt but used incorrectly, 2 punctuation errors and 1 American English word.

2 Key in the correct version of the file.

3 Save as **Health and Safety** into the Skills Practice folder and print. On your printout mark the corrected words.

Some people using computers complain of discomfort when working, such as soar hands and eyes, or back, shoulder and neck pain. This can be avoided and workers must be aware of what they can do to safeguard there own health.

Sit probably in your chair with your back supported and avoid sitting in a twisted position. Change position from time to time. Stretch your arms, neck and shoulders. Hands should be raised above the keyboard with your elbows at a 90 degree angle and your wrists should be straight, fingers curled slightly.

Look after your eyes. Make sure you're screen is not facing a window or the window is directly behind you. Avoid reflection on the screen – use an anti-glare filter. Dont' look at the screen to intensely fore too long. Adjust the color. Look up and focus into the distance periodically and ensure you blink your eyes.

Vary your tasks so you do not spend too long in one position. Get up from your desk, walk round the office and make sure you take the breaks you are entitled to. If you need advise, cheque with your organisation's health and safety officer.

4 Check your corrections on page 84.

→ Check your knowledge

1 List as many things as you can that you should check when proofreading.

2 Why is it important to check your document for accuracy, correctness and meaning?

You will learn to

- Find and replace
- Copy and paste
- Cut and paste (move)
- Work with more than one document open
- Copy and paste text between documents

In this section you will make more changes to the content of documents, by copying and moving text within a document and between different documents.

Information: Search and Replace (Find and Replace)

Sometimes you may wish to replace a word throughout a document with a different word, e.g. change 'he' to 'she'. Word has a feature called **Find and Replace** that can look through a document to **Find** a word and **Replace** it each time it occurs.

Task 9.1 | Use Find and Replace – Replace All

Method

I   Key in the following text:

MANAGEMENT ANNOUNCEMENT

The management and staff of EO recognise the need to move forward. Over the last two years sales have fallen slightly against increasing competition and steps are being taken to put this right.

It is planned to invest in designer shop fittings to update EO's image and to provide the customer with a modern, welcoming environment. A new display and reception area will feature in all branches and staff will be issued with new uniforms.

A customer survey has shown that more Saturday appointments are wanted and the suggestion of early evening appointments is still under consideration. All staff may be required to work these hours on a rota basis, but of course all staff will be consulted before decisions are made. EO must respond to customer needs if we are to retain our place in the current market.

2   Save the file as **Eye Openers** into a new Section 9 folder.
3   Position cursor at the start of the file and select **Replace** from the **Edit** menu.
4   In **Find what** box, key in **customer** (Figure 9.1).

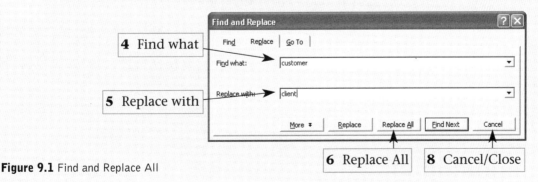

Figure 9.1 Find and Replace All

5 In **Replace with** box, key in **client**.
6 Click on **Replace All**.
7 A message should appear to say that Word has completed its search and found 3 replacements. Click **OK**.
8 Click on **Close** button in Find and Replace window.
9 Save the file and print.

Information

If you choose **Replace** rather than Replace All, Word will stop at each occurrence of the search word and wait for you to replace it.

Task 9.2 Use Find and Replace – Replace

Method

1 Select **Replace** from the **Edit** menu.
2 In **Find what** box, key in **staff**.
3 In **Replace with** box, key in **employees**.
4 Click on **Find next**.
5 Word stops at and highlights the first occurrence of the search word. Click on **Replace** and repeat until a message appears to say that Word has completed its search. Click **OK**.
6 Click on **Close** button in Find and Replace window.
7 Save file as **Eye Openers 2** and print.

Information

Find and Replace has a number of further options (click on **More** in Find and Replace dialogue box), the most common of which is **Match Case**. This is used when replacing a word composed of capital letters. If you do not use it, Word will look for all occurrences of the search word – lower or upper case – and will also replace the matched word with a capitalised word.

Task 9.3 Use Find and Replace – Match case

Remember:

Upper case is capital letters. Lower case is small letters.

Method

1 Select **Replace** from the **Edit** menu.
2 In **Find what** box, key in **EO** (Figure 9.2).

More/Less

Match case

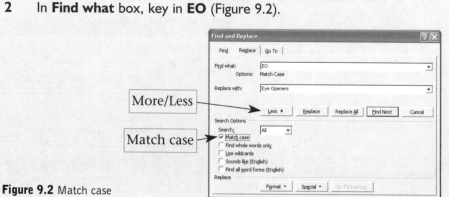

Figure 9.2 Match case

3   In **Replace with** box, key in **Eye Openers**.
4   Click on **More** for options. (Changes to **Less**.)
5   Click in **Match case** box to check on (a tick appears).
6   Click on **Replace All**.
7   A message should appear to say that Word has completed its search. Click **OK**.
8   Click on **Close** button in Find and Replace window.
9   Save file as **Eye Openers 3** and print.

Hint:

Always save a file before printing.

Information: Copy and paste – Cut and paste

You have already used **Copy and Paste** to copy a graphical image (page 57) and you can also do this with text, not only within a document but also between documents. Using the same processes, text or graphics can be **moved** by **cutting** (or removing) them and **pasting** them elsewhere.

When you copy or cut text or graphics, they are held in an area of memory called the **clipboard** until you are ready to paste them out in their new position.

- **Copy and paste** leaves the original in place and creates a duplicate.
- **Cut and paste** removes the original and pastes it in the specified position.

Task 9.4   Copy and paste a word

Method

I   Using the open file **Eye Openers 3**, highlight the word **designer** in the first line of the second paragraph.

Figure 9.3 Cut, copy and paste

2   Click on the **Copy** button (Figure 9.3).
3   Position the cursor directly in front of the word **uniforms** in the last line of the same paragraph.
4   Click on the **Paste** button.

Task 9.5   Copy and paste a text block

Method

I   Highlight the last sentence ending ... **current market**.
2   Click on **Copy**.
3   Position cursor directly after the heading (to the right of **ANNOUNCEMENT**).
4   Press Enter twice.
5   Click on **Paste**.

Hint:

If you have unexpected results, click on Undo ↰ .

Task 9.6 — Cut and paste a text block (move text)

Method

1   Highlight the second paragraph – and the space below it (Figure 9.4). This saves having to adjust the line spacing afterwards.

> Eye Openers must respond to client needs if we are to retain our place in the current market.
>
> The management and employees of Eye Openers recognise the need to move forward. Over the last two years sales have fallen slightly against increasing competition and steps are being taken to put this right.
>
> It is planned to invest in designer shop fittings to update Eye Opener's image and to

Figure 9.4 Highlight text

2   Click on the **Cut** button.
3   Position the cursor at the end of the file after the final full stop.
4   Press Enter twice.
5   Click on **Paste** button. Text should be pasted in position with correct line spacing.
6   Insert a picture of an eye from the clip art gallery on the right-hand side of the first paragraph, applying square text wrap.
7   Save the file as **Eye Openers 4** and print.

Information: Working with more than one document open

So far you have worked with only one document open at a time, but you may often be working on more than one document at once and may also want to copy information between them. When several documents are open, imagine them in a pile, one on top of the other. When you want to work on a particular one, you must bring it to the top.

Task 9.7 — Move between open documents

Method 1

1   Open the file **Eye Openers 4** if not already open.

2   Open a new document

3   Click on the Window menu. It should look similar to Figure 9.5. The current document (the one in front) has a tick beside it.

4   Click on the second document **Eye Openers 4**. It should come to the front.

5   Click on Window menu again and bring the other document to the front.

Figure 9.5 Window menu

Method 2

I Look at the taskbar at the bottom of the screen (Figure 9.6). The name of the current document appears to be 'pressed in'.

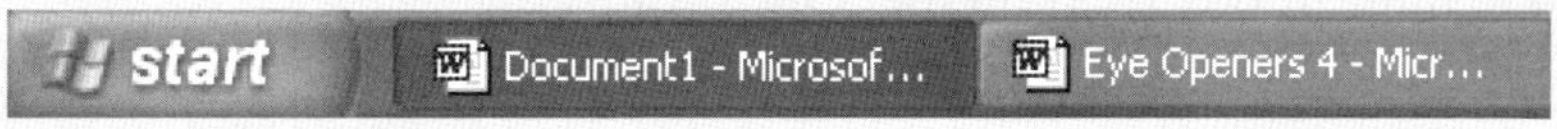

start [W] Document1 - Microsof... [W] Eye Openers 4 - Micr...

Figure 9.6 Taskbar

2 Click on **Eye Openers** 4.
3 Switch back to the other file by clicking on the filename.
4 Close all files.

Use whichever method you prefer. (Method 2 is used also for working with open files from different programs.)

Task 9.8   **Copy and paste between documents**

In this task you will copy a text block and an image from one file to the other.

Method

1 Open **Eye Openers** 4 and a new document.
2 In the new document, key in the heading **STAFF NOTICE** and press **Enter** twice.
3 Save the file into Section 9 folder as **Staff Notice**.
4 Move to **Eye Openers** 4.
5 Highlight the paragraph beginning **It is planned . . .** including the line space below.
6 Click on **Copy** button.
7 Move to the **Staff Notice** document and ensure cursor is positioned one clear line space below the heading.
8 Click on **Paste** button.
9 Add a new paragraph **Plans and uniform designs will be available for discussion at Friday's meeting**.
10 Move back to **Eye Openers** 4.
11 Select the image and click on **Copy**.
12 Move back to **Staff Notice**.
13 Click on **Paste** button. Move image to bottom centre of page.
14 Embolden the heading.
15 Save the file, print. Close all files.

Note: When copying text between files make sure that the fonts and sizes are consistent and correct for the new document.

→ Practise your skills 1

1 Open a new file. Key in the heading **Safety for You**.
2 Save the file as **Safety for You** in the Skills Practice folder.
3 Open the file **Working Safely** stored in My Documents and copy all the text except the heading.
4 Switch to **Safety for You** and paste the text in below the heading.
5 Open the file **Health and Safety** saved in the Skills Practice folder and copy all the text.

6 Switch to **Safety for You**.

7 Position cursor at end of file and ensure there is a line space after the last paragraph. Paste text.

8 Embolden the heading and change to size 16.

9 Change all text to a suitable sans serif font.

10 Insert a suitable piece of clip art, apply **square** text wrap and size to a height of 4 cm, keeping it in proportion. Position it in the bottom left corner of the page.

11 Copy the image and reduce the copy to a size of 2 cm high. Position this in the top right corner.

12 Spellcheck and proofread.

13 Preview the page and adjust the margins all round so the body of text is centred on the page. The images should be within the text and not in the margin area.

14 Insert a page number showing page totals.

15 Save, print **Safety for You** and close all files.

→ Practise your skills 2

1 Open **Safety for You** from the Skills Practice folder.

2 Use Find and Replace to replace **screen** with **monitor**.

3 Save as **Safety for You 2** and print.

→ Practise your skills 3

1 Open a new file and key in the following:

When applying for a new job, the first impression given to your prospective employer is made by your letter of application and your cv. It is therefore important to make the right impression. Your cv lists information about you, for example your address and date of birth. It lists your qualifications including those gained at school and any gained following that, either at college or in the workplace. These are displayed in date order. A cv will show your employment history starting with your most recent position.

2 Save as **CV** and print.

3 Use Find and Replace to replace **cv** with **curriculum vitae**.

4 Save as **Curriculum Vitae** into the Skills Practice folder, print and close.

→ Check your knowledge

1 What is the purpose of Search and Replace (Find and Replace)?

2 What is the difference between Replace All and Replace?

3 When would you use Match case?

4 What is the clipboard?

5 What is the difference between copy and paste, and cut and paste?

6 What is the window menu used for?

Section 10 | Identify and prepare documents

You will learn to

- Identify different documents
- Prepare to produce documents
- Sketch and produce draft document layouts

Information: Documents

There are many different types of document that you may come across and for this qualification you need to be able to identify, though not necessarily produce, some of them.

- Business letters
- Memos
- Forms
- Fax cover sheets
- Newsletters
- Reports
- Promotional material – advertisements, flyers and leaflets.

Most documents are produced on A4 portrait paper, as this is the general-purpose, standard size most commonly available, and which fits all printers. Professional promotional material would be an exception.

- **Business letters** are formal documents and may often be the only contact an organisation has with those outside of it, e.g. its customers. For that reason they must always be accurate and well presented. Letters have a fairly standard layout but this may vary according to the preferred housestyle of an organisation. Housestyle may dictate layout, including margins, as well as fonts and font sizes. Letters are nearly always prepared on A4 portrait paper using a fully blocked style, which means that each line starts at the left margin. Features of a standard business letter are shown in **example A**.

- **Memos** (or memoranda) are used for internal communication within an organisation. They may be created entirely on a word processor or they are sometimes handwritten on a prepared memo form, on A4 portrait or A5 landscape. Margins will be narrower on A5 than A4. Standard headings are used, such as To/From/Date/Subject, in a fully blocked style. When inserting names, titles such as Mr/ Miss are not necessary. Nowadays memos are used less, as e-mail is used more and more. See **examples B** and **C**.

- **Forms** are documents that require people to write on to fill in information. They range from being quite complicated to fairly simple, like the memo form example C. If asked to produce simple forms, always ensure there is sufficient space for people to write in the required information. Paper size and orientation will depend on the size and use of the form. See **examples D** and **E**.

Example A — Business letter (left)

Springfield Business Centre
Oxford
Oxon
OX19 9JJ

Address and contact details

Logo

Tel   01865 923674
Fax   01865 923677

welcome@qdesigns.co.uk
www.qdesign.sco.uk

Managing Director – Richard Egram

Ref: RE/GJ/784 — *Reference*

14 August 2002 — *Date*

The Manager — *Addressee*
Service Department
CopyQuick
145 Parkway Estate
OXFORD OX1 3FD

Dear Sir — *Salutation*

MAINTENANCE CONTRACT 3750 — *Subject heading*

I refer to my letter dated 4 July 2002 and enclose a copy of our agreement. As you are aware, our maintenance contract is coming up for renewal very shortly. For some time now we have been concerned about the level of support we have been getting from your organisation and the delay in response to our requests for repair.

Would you please contact me with a view to arranging a mutually convenient appointment when we can hopefully resolve these problems.

Main body of letter

Yours faithfully — *Complimentary close*

When letter begins Dear Sir or Dear Madam, the letter closes with Yours faithfully

When the letter begins with a name, e.g. Dear Mr Brown, the letter closes with Yours sincerely

Richard Egram
Managing Director

Enc — *Enclosure - if attachments are included*

Example A Business letter

Example B — Memo (right)

MEMO

To   Jenni Foster

Cc   Alain Degas

From   David Portman

Date   5 September 2002

Subject   **Carisbrooke Project**

Now that the Carisbrooke Project is nearly complete, could you plan a celebratory event to take place when it is accepted and signed off? Staff have worked really hard on this project and I want to show our appreciation. Have you got any ideas?

Example B Memo

Example C — Memo

ALG plc   **MEMO**

To	Fergal Roberts
From	Philip Lee
Copies to	Hywell Jones, Carrie Hobson
Date	10 August 2002
Subject	Sales Meeting
Message	Please make sure all your sales reps attend this month's meeting as we want their views on the new commission scheme. If they don't come, they can't moan about it later!

Example C Memo

Example D — Order form

KF   **ORDER FORM**
       ISSUE 27
       MARCH 2002

Kevin Francis from Peggy Davies Ceramics

28 Liverpool Road, Stoke-on-Trent, ST4 1BJ. Tel. 01782 848002 Fax: 01782 747651

I would like to order the following:

1   BRIEF ENCOUNTER

Limited Edition of 500. Modelled by Andy Moss

I enclose either:

An advance payment of £175.50 each
(inclusive of 10% discount for advance payment in full) ☐
Or a deposit of £65 each (full price £195) ☐
Or a Guild payment of £165.75 (inclusive of 15% discount) ☐

Guild Membership No.
(Please allow 28 days for delivery)

ORDER NUMBER	DATE PIECE SENT
DATE ORDER RECEIVED	METHOD OF DESPATCH
DATE CONFIRMATION SENT	

2   MOON DANCE

Limited edition of 750 Modelled by Andy Moss

I enclose either:

An advance payment of £175.50 each
(inclusive of 10% discount for advance payment in full) ☐
Or a deposit of £65 each (full price £195) ☐
Or a Guild payment of £165.75 (inclusive of 15% discount) ☐

Guild Membership No.
(Please allow 28 days for delivery)

Office use only
ORDER NUMBER	DATE PIECE SENT
DATE ORDER RECEIVED	METHOD OF DESPATCH
DATE CONFIRMATION SENT	

3   GUILD MEMBERSHIP

Please remember to tick the appropriate boxes!

I would like to renew my membership of The Kevin Francis Collectors Guild ☐

Guild Membership Number
(The Annual Subscription is due 1st October)

I would like to join the Kevin Francis Collectors Guild for the first time ☐
(The Annual Subscription is due 1st October)

I would like the free mini Toby ☐ or free mini Figurine ☐ or both ☐ (in which case add £40)

£40 ☐   £80 ☐   £40 ☐
Membership   Membership plus   Additional extra mini
             extra mini   when Membership not due

TOTAL £ [   ]

Title ....
First Names ....
Surname ....
Address ....
....
....
....
Post Code ....
Tel. No. ....

Office use only
DATE RECEIVED

DATE FORWARDED

I enclose a cheque ☐ or please debit my account:

VISA ☐ MASTERCARD ☐ AMEX ☐ SWITCH ☐ EUROCARD ☐

Card No. [ ][ ][ ][ ]
Expiry Date [ ][ ]   Switch Issue No [ ]

Signature ....

Example D Order form

Example E — Parking permit form

Parking permit

Staff Parking is very limited on the Broadlands site and there is a waiting list for permits.

Please fill in the form below and your name will be added to the waiting list.

Name ....

Department ....

Extension Number ....

Registration No ....

Date of application ....

Signed ....

Application received by ....

Date ....

Example E Parking permit form

- **Fax cover sheets** are completed and sent by fax with or without accompanying documents. They might be completed entirely by word processing or the details may be completed by hand. They are usually produced on A4 portrait. See **example F**.

Southways Business Park
Fulworth
Reading
Berks
RG1 6TR

Faraday
Wholesale
Supplies

Tel 01764 234126
Fax: 01764 234125

Proprietor P Faraday

FAX TRANSMISSION

Date	
To	
Fax No	
From	
Subject	
No of pages including this page	
Message	

Example F Fax sheet

- **Newsletters** are produced by an organisation for its employees, customers or members and will range from a professional glossy document to an informal sheet produced by a local club or charity. They may be used to give news about an organisation and its products and services, including news stories about staff or members, or bring readers up to date with the latest happenings. Newsletters are usually arranged in columns and may incorporate photographs, clip art, different fonts, borders and other layout features. A4 portrait paper will normally be used. See **examples G** and **H**.

Example G College newsletter

Example H Charity newsletter

- **Reports** may be written at regular intervals to give information, such as a monthly sales report. An **information report** might be informal. See **example I**. Another type of report is written specially as a result of an investigation into a particular subject. Both types of report are divided into paragraphs under headings. An **investigation report** would be more formal and include headings such as Findings, Conclusions and Recommendations. Reports are generally on A4 portrait paper.

Example I Information report

REPORT ON CLIENT COMMENTS

Last month people attending training courses were asked to complete a feedback questionnaire. These results are summarised as follows:

1   PLUS POINTS

Most clients were very pleased with the standard of the training booklets and they were all impressed with their trainer except for some comments about the Supervisors Course.

Specific comments were:

- Impressive training facilities
- Excellent refreshments
- Helpful staff
- Punctual start and finish times

2   MINUS POINTS

There were several comments about the Supervisors course where clients were unable to hear the speaker. There were some sound problems on the day and all clients attending that course have been offered an apology and explanation and offered a 50% reduction off another course.

Specific comments were:

- Too long to wait for coffee during break
- Car parking was difficult

CONCLUSIONS

Generally clients are very happy with their courses. All sound systems must be thoroughly serviced and a spare system should be purchased. Refreshments must arrive on time. The car parking situation must be monitored.

R Waterman
24 August 2002

- **Promotional material** will take many forms, including advertisements, flyers and leaflets. **Advertisements** can be produced in many different sizes, from small column displays in newspapers to full page spreads. Sometimes the same layout is used and simply reduced or increased in size. A **flyer** is an A4 or A5, single or double-sided sheet. It is often found loose inside newspapers, advertising a car insurance company for example, or on your doormat, advertising such services as the local carpet cleaner!
Leaflets will contain more information than a flyer and may be a single sheet of A4 folded into two, or often folded into three. See **examples J** (**advertisements**), **K (flyer)** and **L (leaflet)**.

Example J Advertisements

SPRING OFFERS

FANTASTIC VALUE
10% OFF 3, 4 & 7 NIGHT BREAKS
April 29-May 31st 2002 From £288
ARE YOU A GROUP OF 3 OR LESS? From £270
Quote Ref: MA01S

*May 2 Night Weekend
Breaks From £25 pppn**

SUMMER CHAMPAGNE BREAKS
June 6 - July 5 2002 Inclusive
Book Before May 9th 2002 and qualify for a
complimentary bottle of champagne on arrival!
Quote Ref: MA01S

OUR LUXURIOUSLY FURNISHED COTTAGES CAN ACCOMMODATE UP TO 8 GUESTS AND PRICES INCLUDE
V.A.T, LINEN, TOWELS AND FULL USE OF OUR OWN LEISURE CENTRE, JUST A MINUTE'S WALK FROM
YOUR FRONT DOOR.

PLEASE CALL RESERVATIONS TODAY ON
0800 262 902

ALL OFFERS ARE SUBJECT TO AVAILABILITY AND CANNOT BE USED IN CONJUNCTION WITH ANY OTHER
OFFER AVAILABLE AT TIME OF BOOKING.

*BASED ON FULL OCCUPANCY

Example K Flyer

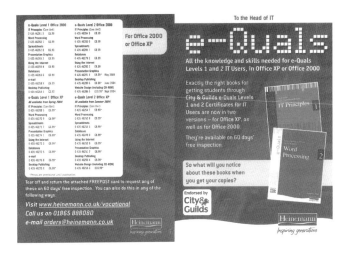

Example L Leaflet

Hint:

When creating your new folder, ensure the Save in: box reads My Documents.

Task 10.1 Produce a letter

Reproduce the letter, **example A** (page 70). Use appropriate size and orientation of paper with suitable margins. Use clip art or WordArt as a logo. Save with a suitable name into a new Section 10 folder.

Task 10.2 Produce a memo

Reproduce the memo, **example B** (page 70). Use appropriate size and orientation of paper with suitable margins. Set a tab at 3 cm to line up addressee, date etc. Use clip art or WordArt as a logo. Save with a suitable name into the Section 10 folder.

Task 10.3 Produce a memo form

Reproduce the memo form, **example C** (page 70). Use appropriate size and orientation of paper with suitable margins. Use clip art or WordArt as a logo. Ensure you leave sufficient space for handwritten text. Save with a suitable name into the Section 10 folder.

Task 10.4 Produce a form

Reproduce the parking permit form, **example E** (page 70). Use appropriate size and orientation of paper with suitable margins. Ensure you leave sufficient space for handwritten text. Save with a suitable name into the Section 10 folder.

Task 10.5 — Produce a fax cover sheet

Reproduce the fax cover sheet, **example F** (page 71). Ensure you leave sufficient space for handwritten text. Save with a suitable name into the Section 10 folder.

Task 10.6 — Produce a short report

Reproduce the report, **example I** (page 72). Use appropriate size and orientation of paper with suitable margins. Select fonts and font size. Use bullets where indicated but do not use the numbering button – type the numbers in. Save with a suitable name into the Section 10 folder.

Information: Planning and preparing to produce new documents

When asked to produce a document you will often be given information with which to prepare it. This might be handwritten text, text to be copied from another word processed document, numerical data or graphics. Before starting, you must make sure you have everything you need:

- Check you have any handwritten text you need.
- Locate any word processed file you need to copy from.
- Locate any numerical data you need – is it a printout or is it stored in a file?

In your test, you may be asked to sketch a draft layout for a document, though you may not have to reproduce it. Drawing sketches before you start can help you to think about what you need to do, rather than rush on and do it and make mistakes. Sketching helps you to plan your document and consider the layout. A sketch for the fax cover sheet above might look like this:

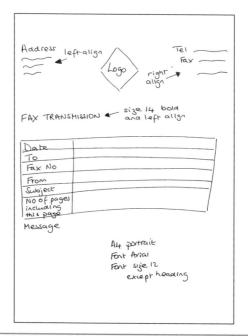

Task 10.7   Prepare a document

You work for Neil Harrison, Manager of the local leisure centre. Read his note below:

> *You produced a list of the pool opening hours a while ago that is needed for a notice to be put on the boards around the centre. Could you find it and then prepare a draft notice.*
>
> *Head the notice PLEASE NOTE NEW POOL OPENING HOURS and add the following:*
>
> *The Management are pleased to announce new extended opening hours for the pool complex. See below.*
>
>   *Insert table here with gridlines.*
>
> *Don't forget – the new monthly memberships at £12.50 for adults and £8.50 for children give unlimited sessions! Sign up NOW!*
>
> *One or two clip art images to illustrate the notice would be a good idea.*

1   Locate the file you produced called Pool Opening Times and print it out. Write on your printout which folder it was stored in.

2   Find two suitable clip art images for the notice and print them out.

3   Select a suitable paper size and orientation and produce a sketch of the notice.

4   Indicate where the main heading will be and the text.

5   Draw the table showing rough widths of columns.

6   Indicate where the images will be positioned.

7   Write on the sketch which fonts, font sizes, and line spacing you will use and any text enhancement, e.g. use of bold etc.

8   Now create the notice. Proofread and preview.

9   Adjust layout as necessary and print.

10   Check the printout and adjust again if necessary. Save with a suitable name into the Section 10 folder.

You are working part-time for a garden centre and you have been asked to produce a draft A5 flyer to be delivered with the local free paper. The information is below.

Ashworth Garden Centre
Purley Road
Ashworth

Spring Offers

Prepare your garden for the summer

Perennials
Annuals
Hanging baskets
Shrubs
Pots
Gifts

Open every day from 8 – 6
Sundays 10 – 4

Demonstrations at the weekend
Bring along the family

---

1   Before creating this flyer you must produce a sketch showing the layout, position of graphics, fonts, font sizes, use of bold, italics, underline, alignment, line spacing and use of bullets.

Instructions for layout:

2   Use any sans serif font.

3   Garden centre name in 20 bold and centred.

4   Address size 16 and centred.

5   Spring Offers in size 36 centred.

6   Use bullets for the list of 6 items.

7   Use double line spacing for the bulleted list only.

8   Indent bulleted list by 2 cm.

9   All other text should be centred and size 14.

10 Include 2 or 3 clip art images.

11 Produce the flyer, proofread, preview and adjust margins and layout as necessary.

12 Print and check, readjusting if necessary.

13 Save using a suitable name into Skills Practice folder.

Note: Check your sketch with the example on page 85.

→ Practise your skills 2

1 You have promised an article for the next company newsletter Locate the file **Feng Shui** stored in one of your folders.

2 Prepare the following memo to send to Henri Fontaine from yourself and date it today. Use a serif font other than Times New Roman throughout.

3 Use WordArt to create a logo with the letters **KLP** and place in the top right corner.

4 The subject heading is **Article for Newsletter**.

5 The message is:
Here is the article you wanted for this month's newsletter.

6 Copy the text and images from the Feng Shui file into the memo.

7 Ensure the font and size matches the rest of the memo.

8 Proofread and adjust if necessary.

9 Save with a suitable name in Skills Practice folder.

10 Print.

→ Check your knowledge

1 What is a fully blocked style?

2 A memo is used for communication with customers. True or False?

3 What is a flyer?

4 What is a report?

5 What might you expect to find in a newsletter?

6 What features might you expect to see in a business letter, e.g. date?

7 What is the mostly commonly used size and orientation of paper used?

8 When preparing to create a document what should you do?

9 What is the purpose of drawing sketches?

10 When creating a form that needs to be filled in by hand, what must you remember to do?

Practice assignments

There now follows two practice assignments which cover the skills you have acquired. These follow the format of the actual assignment for which you are allowed two hours to complete. Worked examples appear on pages 86–88. Good luck!

Practice assignment 1

Scenario
You work in the general office of Lakeside Holidays. Some special offers have been worked out to attract existing customers to come again for weekend breaks later in the year. You have been asked to produce a notice to be displayed around the holiday site.

Task A

1 Read the scenario.

2 Open a new word processor file and enter the following text:

Lakeside Holidays

Enjoyed your holiday here at Lakeside?
If so, why not come back later

Weekend Breaks

Murder Mystery Weekend
60s Theme Weekend
Talent Contest Weekend
Halloween Special
Bonfire Bonanza
Turkey and Tinsel Breaks

Special Offers available now

15% off if you book before you go home
10% off if you book later

Call in at Reception any time

---

3 Change the page setup to A5 portrait.

4 Use a serif font throughout.

5 Use bold and font size 28 for the main heading.

6 Use 24 bold for Weekend Breaks.

7 Use font size 14 for all remaining text.

8   Use bullets for the list of 6 weekend breaks.

9   Indent the bulleted list 1.5 cm.

10 Put the bulleted list into double line spacing.

11 Centre all text apart from the bulleted list.

12 Put the lines starting **15% off ...** and **10% off ...** into italics and embolden them.

13 Embolden **Special Offers available now** and increase size to 20.

14 Underline the last line.

15 Insert two suitable pieces of clip art and position.

16 Proofread carefully.

17 Preview the page and balance margins.

18 Save as WEEKEND DEALS.

19 Make a backup copy by saving also to floppy disk as WEEKEND BACKUP.

20 Print.

Task B

1   An entry form is needed for the weekly talent contest.

2   Reproduce the form on A4 portrait paper using a 2-column table.

3   Use a sans serif font and format the text as you think fit.

4   Space it appropriately.

LAKESIDE HOLIDAYS

TALENT CONTEST ENTRY FORM

Name	
Chalet Number	
Under 12	
12-18	
Adult	
Singer	
Dancer	
Comedy	
Other (please state)	

Please enter my name for the talent contest on Thursday evening.

Signed ....

Signature of parent if aged under 18 ....

---

5   Position the initials LH in the bottom right of the page in Arial size 48 bold.

6   Proofread your work carefully.

7   Preview the page and balance the form on the page.

8   Save as TALENT CONTEST.

9   Print.

Practice assignment 2

Scenario
You are working for the Crossways Hotel chain in the administration
office. Your employer has left you a note.

We really need a new form for guests to fill in regarding their views on the
services we offer. Could you draw a sketch of the form using the following
information:

> *Guest Questionnaire*
>
> *We value your custom and hope you will return. In order to help us offer the
> best possible service, please complete the following form.*
>
> *<Insert the table here>*
>
> *Thank you. We are grateful for your time and look forward to seeing you soon.*
>
> *Sonia Johnson*
> *Manager*

The table should be a 5-column table with 7 rows. These are the column
headings:

Area of service, Excellent, Good, Average, Poor

Below Area of service in the first column, list the following:

Reservations
Reception and Check-in
Room Cleanliness
Room Comfort
Restaurant
Helpfulness of staff

Thanks

Task A

1   Prepare a sketch first for A5 landscape paper.
2   A sans serif font is required throughout.
3   Right align the Manager's name and title.
4   Format the heading as 28 point bold.
5   Use suitable widths for the columns and row heights.
6   When you are happy with your sketch, open a new file and create the form.

7 Proofread carefully.

8 Preview the page and balance the margins.

9 Save as QUESTIONNAIRE and print.

Task B

Please prepare a letter as a sample to be sent out to guests.

Mr J Gustafsen
23 Fielding Way
Wilsham
Leeds
LS19 5FG

Today's date

Dear Mr Gustafsen

CUSTOMER SURVEY

You recently stayed at our Stoke-on-Trent hotel and we very much hope that you
enjoyed your stay.

We are always striving to offer the very best of service to our customers and in
order to help us do this we hope you will complete the form below and return it to
us. To show our appreciation, if you return this form we will send you by return, a
discount voucher for your next stay.

Yours sincerely

Sonia Johnson
Manager

✂...

Name ....

Date of stay ....

<insert table here>

1 At the end of the letter, copy the table from the QUESTIONNAIRE file
   that you have just created.

2 Make sure the same sans serif font is used throughout the letter.

3 Make the heading bold.

4 Proofread and spellcheck.

5 Print preview and balance the margins.

6 Save as CUSTOMER LETTER.

7 Print.

Solutions

Section 1 Getting started

Check your knowledge

1 The file name.
2 When a word would extend beyond the margin, Word automatically starts a new line.
3 Press Enter twice to leave a blank line.
4 Use a name that reflects the contents so you can locate it later.
5 Press down the Caps Lock.
6 Click on File menu, select New, select Blank Document or click on

New Blank Document button

7 Alt Gr + 4.
8 In the blue title bar at the top of the screen.
9 One or two – but be consistent.
10 Hard copy is a printout of a file. Soft copy is the onscreen version.

Section 2 Editing

Check your knowledge

1 Editing (text) means to change the words in a document, by deleting, inserting, copying or moving.
2 Save every ten minutes, before printing and after making significant changes. If a system error or a power failure should occur you would only lose your work up until you last saved.
3 When saving a file for the first time you must name it. Subsequently using Save will save an amended file replacing the original. Save As allows you to give a file a new name or save to a new location.
4 Use Save once you have named a file and to save a file at regular intervals as you work. Use Save As to save a new version of a file with a new name or to another location but keeping the original version intact.
5 Press the Home key.
6 It only recognises words in the in-built dictionary. It does *not* recognise proper names, spot words used in the wrong context, e.g. their/there, check for sense or meaning.
7 To make paragraph and space markers visible for editing and checking purposes.
8 When overtype mode is on, text keyed in will overwrite existing text at the cursor point. When it is off, new text can be keyed in and existing text will move to the right.
9 Both delete text but Backspace deletes to the left of the cursor position and Delete to the right.
10 **a** Open new file   **b** Open existing file   **c** Save file   **d** Print

Section 3 Selecting and formatting

Check your knowledge

1 Double click on the word.
2 Highlighted.
3 To change the appearance of text.
4 Depends – probably Times New Roman size 12.
5 Text with straight left and right margins.
6 Left aligned.
7 10–12.
8 Serif fonts have strokes at the ends of characters. Sans serif fonts do not.
9 Arial.
10 Check your list against Format text – Text styles and enhancement (page 19) and Format text – Text alignment (page 22).

Section 4 Saving and opening files using specified locations

Check your knowledge

1 The hard disk of a single standalone computer.
2 The floppy disk drive.
3 To store related files and to make it easier to find files later.
4 The disk drive light to go out.
5 A duplicate copy of a file in case something happens to the original.

Section 5 Tables and lists

Check your knowledge

1 Decimal tab.
2 Centre tab.
3 Right tab.
4 Left tab.
5 Highlight text and drag tab marker downwards from ruler.
6 Press the tab key.
7 Highlight numbered list and click on Bullets button.
8 Drag the column boundary to left or right.
9 Border button – for adding and removing borders.
10 Highlight table, click on Borders button, select No Borders.

Section 6 Page formatting and layout

Check your knowledge

1 A4 portrait.
2 What You See Is What You Get – What you see on the screen is what you get on your printout.
3 It gives you a chance to adjust features such as margins and font size, preview multiple pages, check the appearance of long documents to ensure consistency and layout, fine-tune page breaks, reposition graphics to achieve balance.
4 Letters, memos, advertising flyers, forms, reports, booklets, newsletters.

5 The right margin should not normally be wider than the left although they may be equal, and the top margin should not be bigger than the bottom, as the page can look unbalanced. Margins for A5 will generally be narrower.

6 This is most useful for fitting a document onto one page if a few lines of text spill over onto another page, by reducing the size of the text.

7 Use Indent toolbar button or Format menu – Paragraph.

8 A soft page break is automatically inserted when text reaches the bottom margin. It will adjust with any editing made. A hard break is inserted by you and remains in a fixed position.

9 An option for preventing a single line appearing at the top or bottom of a page, separated from the rest of a paragraph.

10 It ensures logical reading order, easy re-assembly if pages mixed up and serves as reference point. Page totals ensure that the reader knows how many pages there should be.

Section 7 Inserting graphics

Check your knowledge

1 Always use a corner handle to resize an image.

2 They can be used to illustrate the text making it more interesting to look at.

3 It ensures the image is kept in proportion when resizing to a specific size and not distorted.

4 Text wrapping.

5 It makes it difficult to read the text because the reader's eyes would have to jump over the image to read the end of the line.

Section 8 Proofreading

Practise your skills 1

12 errors

1 The Norwegian holiday promised a cruise around <u>fiords</u> in and out around the
2 <u>the</u> small islands and calling at picture postcard fishing villages and deserted
3 bays. The scenery <u>shows</u> a <u>market</u> contrast between the <u>breath-taking</u>
4 mountains and the little <u>colorful</u> villages. There was also the chance to make
5 the never-forgotten visit to the 'The Kingdom <u>for</u> the <u>Wales</u>' to see
6 <u>magnificient</u> black and white orcas. All this – 7 days and nights for only <u>£473</u>.

Practise your skills 2

Some people using computers complain of discomfort when working, such as <u>sore</u> hands and eyes, or back, shoulder and neck pain. This can be avoided and workers must be aware of what they can do to safeguard <u>their</u> own health.

Sit <u>properly</u> in your chair with your back supported and avoid sitting in a twisted position. Change position from time to time. Stretch your arms, neck and shoulders. Hands should be raised above the keyboard with your elbows at a 90 degree angle and your wrists should be straight, fingers curled slightly.

Look after your eyes. Make sure <u>your</u> screen is not facing a window or the window is directly behind you. Avoid reflection on the screen – use an anti-glare filter. <u>Don't</u> look at the screen <u>too</u> intensely <u>for</u> too long. Adjust the <u>colour</u>. Look up and focus into the distance periodically and ensure you blink your eyes.

Vary your tasks so you do not spend too long in one position. Get up from your desk, walk round the office and make sure you take the breaks you are entitled to. If you need <u>advice</u>, <u>check</u> with your organisation's health and safety officer.

Check your knowledge

1 See list on page 61.
2 See first three paragraphs on page 61.

Section 9 Further editing

Check your knowledge

1 To search through a document for a word and replace it with another.
2 Replace All automatically replaces the word each time it occurs. Replace waits for you to confirm replacement.
3 To find and match words in capital letters.
4 An area of memory where text and images are held when using cut or paste, until you are ready to paste them out in their new position.
5 Copy and Paste leaves the original in place and creates a duplicate. Cut and Paste removes the original and pastes it in the required position.
6 It allows you to move between open files.

Section 10 Identify and prepare documents

Practise your skills 1

Check your knowledge

1 Each line starts at the left margin.
2 False. It is used for communication *within* an organisation.
3 A single sheet promoting goods or services, often tucked inside newspapers and magazines or posted through your door.
4 A document written to provide information on a subject or as a result of an investigation.
5 News about an organisation and its products and services; news stories about staff or members.
6 Contact details, logo, date, reference, addressee, salutation, subject, main body of letter, complimentary close. Enc if there is an enclosure.
7 A4 portrait.
8 Check you have everything you need, e.g. handwritten text, stored files, numerical information and images.
9 It helps you to think about what you need to do rather than rush on, and make mistakes. It helps you to plan your document and consider the layout.
10 Leave enough space for people to write in.

Practice assignments

Practice assignment 1

Task A

Lakeside Holidays

Enjoyed your holiday here at Lakeside?
If so, why not come back later

Weekend Breaks

- Murder Mystery Weekend

- 60s Theme Weekend

- Talent Contest Weekend

- Halloween Special

- Bonfire Bonanza

- Turkey and Tinsel Breaks

Special Offers available now

15% off if you book before you go home
10% off if you book later

Call in at Reception any time

Task B

LAKESIDE HOLIDAYS
TALENT CONTEST ENTRY FORM

Please enter my name for the talent contest on Thursday evening.

Name	
Chalet Number	
Under 12	
12-18	
Adult	
Singer	
Dancer	
Comedy	
Other (please state)	

Signed . . . .

Signature of parent if aged under 18 . . . .

LH

Practice assignment 2

Task A

GUEST QUESTIONNAIRE — 28 Bold

We value your custom

Area of Service	Excellent	Good	Average	Poor
Reservations				
Reception				
Room Cleanliness				
Room comfort				
Restaurant				
Helpfulness of staff				

Thank you

Tahoma font

Sonia Johnson
Manager
right aligned

Guest Questionnaire

We value your custom and hope you will return. In order to help us offer the best possible service, please complete the following form.

Area of service	Excellent	Good	Average	Poor
Reservations				
Reception and Check-in				
Room Cleanliness				
Room Comfort				
Restaurant				
Helpfulness of staff				

Thank you. We are grateful for your time and look forward to seeing you soon.

Sonia Johnson
Manager

Task B

Mr J Gustafsen
23 Fielding Way
Wilsham
Leeds
LS19 5FG

Today's date

Dear Mr Gustafsen

CUSTOMER SURVEY

You recently stayed at our Stoke-on-Trent hotel and we very much hope that you enjoyed your stay.

We are always striving to offer the very best of service to our customers and in order to help us do this we hope you will complete the form below and return it to us. To show our appreciation, if you return this form we will send you by return, a discount voucher for your next stay.

Yours sincerely

Sonia Johnson
Manager

✂ ....

Name ....

Date of stay ....

Area of service	Excellent	Good	Average	Poor
Reservations				
Reception and Check-in				
Room Cleanliness				
Room Comfort				
Restaurant				
Helpfulness of staff				

Outcomes matching guide

Outcome 1 Plan and prepare new documents		
Practical activities		
1	Produce draft layouts	Section 10
2	Check the required data is available	Section 10
3	Sketch suitable positioning and appearance of the required text and graphics	Section 10
Underpinning knowledge		
1	Identify common types of documents	Section 10
2	Identify the main paper sizes and state their typical uses	Sections 6, 10
3	State how different styles and sizes of fonts can affect the appearance of a document	Section 3
4	State the purpose of text enhancement and when it should be used	Section 3
5	Identify common methods used to structure text	Sections 3, 5, 6
6	State how the use and positioning of graphics can be used to improve the appearance of a document	Section 7
Outcome 2 Produce new documents		
Practical activities		
1	Start the word processing software with a new blank document	Section 1
2	Set up the page layout for a planned document	Sections 6, 10
3	Input the required text with suitable formatting • Alignments • Enhancement • Tabulation • Font size and style • Paragraphs and indentation • Bulleted or numbered lists	Section 3 Section 3 Section 5 Section 3 Section 6 Section 5
4	Copy and paste text from an existing document	Section 9
5	Insert simple graphics	Section 7
6	Insert page breaks	Section 6
7	Insert automatic page numbering	Section 6
Underpinning knowledge		
1	State the difference between hard and soft breaks	Section 6
2	Identify when hard page breaks should be used	Section 6
3	State the importance of page numbering and page totals	Section 6

Outcome 3 Edit existing documents		
Practical activities		
1	Open existing documents for editing from hard disk and floppy disk	Section 4
2	Check existing page layout and change as required	Section 6
3	Edit existing documents by: Selecting (highlighting) Inserting and deleting Copying and pasting Cutting and pasting	Section 3 Section 2 Section 9 Section 9
4	Check the existing text formats and change as required	Sections 3, 5, 9
5	Modify page breaks as required	Section 6
6	Check page numbering and page totals	Section 6
Outcome 4 Check produced documents		
Practical activities		
1	Use a spellchecker on part and whole documents	Sections 2, 3
2	Proofread documents	Section 8
3	Use search and replace to make corrections to whole documents	Section 9
4	Use print preview to check the layout of the finished document and change as required	Section 6
Underpinning knowledge		
1	Identify the limitations of automated spellcheckers	Section 2
2	State the importance of checking documents for accuracy, correctness and meaning	Section 8
3	State the important of checking the layout of the finished document in a wysiwyg display such as Print Preview	Section 6
Outcome 5 Save and print documents		
Practical activities		
1	Save documents with suitable filenames in specified locations	Section 4
2	Make a copy of a document giving it a different name using Save As . . .	Section 2
3	Print check and preview documents	Section 6
4	Check the printed output for accuracy and layout	Section 8
5	Close the finished document and the word processing software	Section 1
Underpinning knowledge		
1	State the difference between Save and Save As	Section 2

Quick reference guide

Action	Button	Menu	Keyboard
Bold	**B**	Format – Font	Ctrl + B
Borders	⊡	Format – Borders and Shading	
Bullets	☰	Format – Bullets and Numbering – Bulleted	
Cancel			Esc
Centre align	≡	Format – Paragraph – Indents and Spacing	Ctrl + E
Close or exit		File – Close or Exit	Alt + F4
Copy	🗐	Edit – Copy	Ctrl + C
Cut	✂	Edit – Cut	Ctrl + X
Decrease indent	⇤	Format – Paragraph – Indents and Spacing	
End of line			End
Exit or close		File – Close or Exit	Alt + F4
Find		Edit – Find	Ctrl + F
Font	Times New Roman ▾	Format – Font – Font	
Font size	12 ▾	Format – Font – Font	
Indent	⇥	Format – Paragraph – Indents and Spacing	Ctrl + M
Insert clip art	🖼 From Drawing toolbar	Insert – Picture – ClipArt	
Italics	*I*	Format – Font – Font	Ctrl + I
Justify	≣	Format – Paragraph – Indents and Spacing	Ctrl + J
Left align	≡	Format – Paragraph – Indents and Spacing	Ctrl + L
Line spacing		Format – Paragraph – Indents and Spacing	Single – Ctrl + 1 1½ – Ctrl + 5 Double – Ctrl + 2
Margins		File – Page Setup – Margins	
New file	▯	File – New	Ctrl + N
Normal View	left of status bar		
Numbering	☰	Format – Bullets and Numbering – Numbered	

Open file		File – Open	Ctrl + O
Page break		Insert – Break – Page Break	Ctrl + Return
Page number		Insert – Page Numbers or View – Header and Footer	
Paper size/ orientation		File – Page Setup – Paper Size	
Paste		Edit – Paste	Ctrl + V
Print		File – Print	Ctrl + P
Print Layout View	left of status bar		
Print preview		File – Print Preview	Ctrl + F2
Redo			
Replace		Edit – Replace	Ctrl + H
Right align		Format – Paragraph – Indents and Spacing	Ctrl + R
Save		File – Save	Ctrl + S
Save As		File – Save As	F12
Select All		Edit – Select All	Ctrl + A
Show/Hide	¶		
Spellcheck		Tools – Spelling and Grammar	F7
Start of line			Home
Symbol		Insert – Symbol	
Switch between files		Window – select file	
Table		Table – Insert – Table	
Tabs	L Select tab type from ruler	Format – Tabs	
Underline	U	Format – Font – Font	Ctrl + U
Undo		Edit – Undo	
WordArt	from Drawing toolbar	Insert – Object – Microsoft WordArt	